fashion Sweatshirts

Lorine Mason

©2004 Lorine Mason

Published by

krause publications
An Imprint of F+W Publications

700 East State Street • Iola, WI 54990-0001
715-445-2214 • 888-457-2873
www.krausebooks.com

Our toll-free number to place an order or obtain a free catalog is 800-258-0929.

The following trademark terms and companies appear in the publication:
2" Quilt Press™, Avery®, Beads-2-Fuse™, Chenille by the Inch™, Chenille Thick & Quick®, Fabri-Tac™, Lion Brand®, Patons®, Red Heart® Hokey Pokey™, Steam-A-Seam 2® and Velcro®.

Library of Congress Catalog Number: 2004113675

ISBN-13: 978-0-87349-912-5
ISBN-10: 0-87349-912-3

Edited by Sarah Herman
Designed by Donna Mummery

Printed in the United States of America

dedication

To Bill, my loving husband, whose acceptance, understanding and unyielding encouragement of my many endeavors throughout our marriage have led me to a career I truly love.

acknowledgments

Growing up in a large family provided me with a wonderful opportunity to share my creative talents. Entertaining siblings with stories, crafts and other activities was just one part of being the oldest daughter and self-appointed caretaker. I would like to thank my parents, Henry and Mildred Schlamp, for nurturing my creative talents throughout my childhood. To my wonderful husband, Bill: You are my cheerleader in life. I am better because of you. My daughters, Jocelyn and Kimbrely, have been along side of me the entire journey. Their love and honesty kept me on track.

I have been very fortunate in my life to have friends who have encouraged my many endeavors. Tina, Eileen, Cheryl, Jan, Regina and Diane, thank you for believing in me. I also count many fellow designers as friends. Debra and Koren, you're the best.

I would like to thank the wonderful people at KP Books, especially Sarah Herman and Julie Stephani. To the many models whose photos grace the pages of this book: Your patience, humor and beauty shine brightly throughout the book. Thank you so much.

contents

foreword

Style and comfort are a winning combination for any wardrobe. In Fashion Sweatshirts, talented designer and good friend Lorine Mason has elevated comfy crewneck sweatshirts to high-fashion jackets and accessories. Combining creative cutting techniques and wonderful embellishments from beads to fancy yarns, each of the more than 25 designs is unique and attractive. From children to adults, Lorine creates fashionable styles for everyone. Step-by-step instructions and photos make the creation of these designs easy with the basic sewing, knitting and other techniques explained fully. Dig out a plain jane sweatshirt and create yourself a beautiful jacket with a matching purse. Get together with friends and daughters and have fun altering sweatshirts together to make colorful, trendy jackets. Lorine brings her stylish design flair to each sweatshirt, transforming it into a stunning and comfortable garment. "Fashion Sweatshirts" is a must-have book for every sewer's library.

Debra Quartermain
Author of "Nursery Decor" and "Easy to Sew Playful Toys"

introduction

The basic sweatshirt that we've all worn at one time or another can be transformed into a unique and exciting new garment. During the mid 1920s, the word "sweatshirt" was introduced into our vocabulary. The early versions were simple, gray pullovers used by athletes to keep them warm before or after sports activities. Creative ideas can turn this same basic wardrobe item into a unique fashion statement with the addition of unusual fabric treatments or decorative embellishments. Think of the sweatshirt as a blank canvas. Use fabric, trims and embellishments as your paint. Add your personal design signature to a simple garment with the variety of embellishments available at local establishments or on the Internet.

The most basic of sewing, knitting, crocheting and embroidery skills are used in the transformation of the sweatshirts in this book. Use these designs and this book as a resource, not necessarily looking for the exact fabric, trim or yarn that I used in a particular design. This book should be a guide, helping you make choices and inspiring you to design your own creations. At times, I chose a particular design, color or weight of fabric with an idea in mind. At other times, it was the embellishment, fabric or yarn that inspired me. You do not have to resort to an array of art and sewing classes to develop innovative ideas and stimulate your own creative resources. Where do you find ideas, creativity, inspiration, or that perfect idea? It varies, but here are some of the ways that I find inspiration.

getting started and finishing touches

Once you learn the basics of creating collars, cuffs, facings and hemlines, you can personalize any sweatshirt. Embellishing is easy with basic knitting, crochet and embroidery stitches.

Creating Inspirational Files

I keep files packed full of torn pieces of paper taken from a variety of sources. Where do I find these ideas? I find them in fashion and home decorating magazines, books, television programs and advertising flyers. Interesting color and pattern combinations, the unusual use of a fabric, or perhaps the embellishment might spark my interest. You can also check out the latest fashions, not only by flipping through the magazines, but by taking a field trip. What is the current rage being pushed by the famous fashion designers? They, too, are constantly challenged with redesigning the classics. The wheel has been invented, therefore let the challenge begin—if you cannot make a better wheel, perhaps it will be a fun or unique wheel! Transfer that thought to sweatshirts and you might come up with a pretty bed jacket or beaded evening jacket. What makes it to my files? I keep everything from paint chips picked up at the home décor store to photos of an interesting neckline or sleeve. One evening while watching television, I took note of an interesting neckline and asymmetrical opening on a blouse a celebrity was wearing. I quickly grabbed a piece of paper and sketched out the basic idea. (I am by no means a sketch artist—a stick figure with the lines drawn will help you visualize my drawing). The idea is not to copy, but to inspire a design. The blouse that originally caught my eye was a plain white, fitted blouse with an asymmetrical line and collar, giving it an Asian influence. The Asian Poppy design is what I created from that inspiration. The only similarity is that they both have an asymmetrical opening, giving it an Asian look. I hope this book will do for you what my file does for me—inspire.

Choosing Fabric

Selecting the fabric brings to mind the old question—which came first, the chicken or the egg? When meandering through the fabric store, take time to not only look, but touch the fabric. Some of my best designs have come from my choice of fabric. The color, texture or print may provide the direction a design travels. A selection of complementary flannel fabrics directed me to put together the design for the Watercolor Garden sweatshirt. Do not forget to check out the home decor aisles as well. Although most home décor fabrics call for dry cleaning, it is usually due to the finish. Check the fabric content. Cotton and cotton blends are washable. Try pre-washing a sample piece to see if you like the washed look. Keep in mind the intended use of the garment when choosing fabrics. Will the garment need cleaning constantly? If so, select fabrics suitable for washing. Pre-wash the fabrics to prevent shrinkage and dye problems later. Generally, I wash and press fabrics prior to sewing in the exact manner I intend to care for the finished item.

the idea

Knitting and Crocheting

The popularity of knitting and crocheting has grown steadily over the past number of years. How did the industry manage to make knitting and crocheting interesting again? One part of the current knitting trend's success is in the yarns available. Take a trip to your neighborhood craft or yarn store and you will know what I am talking about. Novelty yarns in wonderful watercolor combinations, bright, cozy chenilles and eyelash yarns beckon the consumer to touch. I am a basic knitter, but I was hooked as soon as I stopped in the yarn department. I purchased a ball of a variegated curly eyelash yarn without even having a project in mind. The colors, combined with the soft texture, called me to bring it home. I soon discovered that my somewhat limited knitting experience was enough to produce a basic collar, as the yarn shines through with even the simplest of stitches.

Vintage Linens, Buttons and More

Linens and clothing items found in thrift stores can turn into beautifully recycled fabric or trim accents. Check out local thrift stores or perhaps your own closets. Stained or torn items can be recycled into wonderfully unique additions. Perhaps you can make a collar from a torn crocheted doily or pocket accents from a worn, embroidered dresser scarf? I have used vintage (recycled) crocheted doilies in two of my designs. The Photo and Lace and Mosaic Tea Party sweatshirts both feature crocheted trims courtesy of doilies that I have resurrected into collars, trims and simple accents. In some cases, the items were tea dyed or bleached prior to attaching them to the designs. Notice the buttons and trims on thrift and yard sale clothing. I have purchased items simply for the buttons. At times, their use is not clear at the time of purchase, but the thrill of the hunt is inspirational. You can also find your design direction through the embellishments. Keep this in mind the next time you are searching through your own castoffs. Regularly featured articles about collecting antique linens and buttons have made the hunt more of a challenge, but they are still out there. Reproductions of vintage trims and other embellishments are available as well, if you can not find the perfect item.

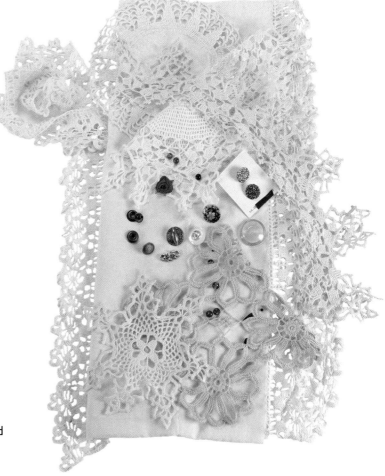

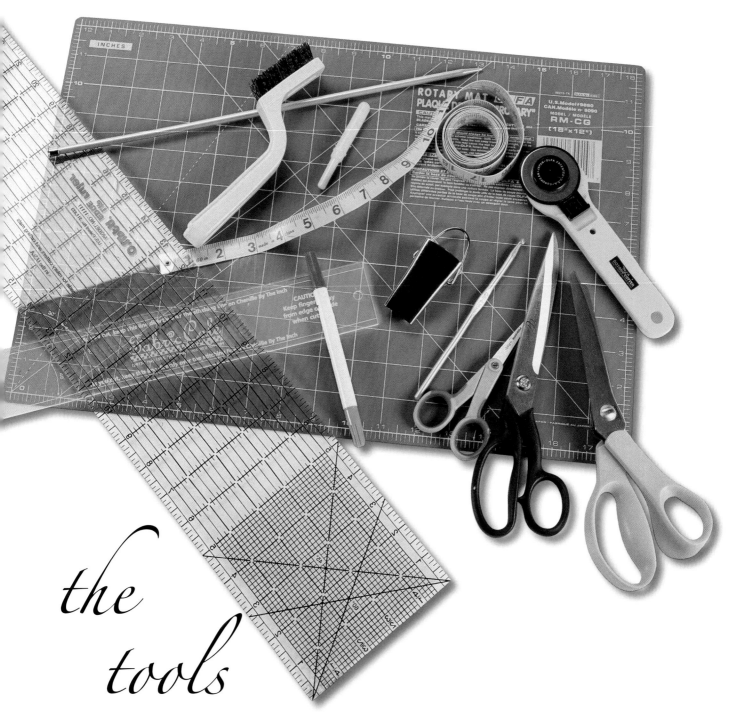

the
tools

Sewing Accessories

New and improved sewing supplies and equipment accessories that save time and help achieve a professional look are easily worth their weight in gold. Basting, cutting, marking and stitching all have tools that can help with some of the more tedious tasks. Some of my favorites, although not new, are a bias tape maker, tube-style cord turner and last, but certainly not least, are the rotary cutter, mats and rulers. There are many brands of fusible web on the market. I have chosen to use Steam-A-Seam 2 Fusible Web Tape and Steam-A-Seam 2 Double Stick Fusible Web throughout the book because of its superior quality. These are products that work for me, but use what works best for you. Time spent browsing through your local sewing store, mail order catalog or Internet sources will be well spent if you discover an item that can save you time or improve your skills. Check out your local fabric stores to see what's new.

Remove the ribbed banding from the sweatshirt.

Straighten the edges after removing the ribbed banding.

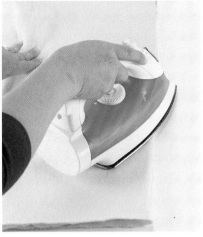

Press the center fold.

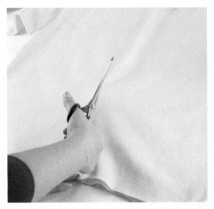

Cut along the fold.

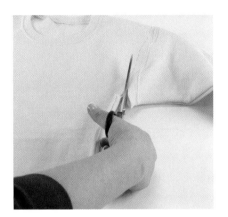

Remove the sleeves by cutting along the seam line.

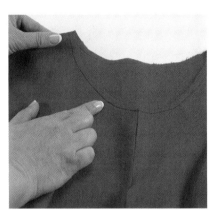

Stay stich all edges.

Creating a Cardigan or Vest

Check the information provided with each design because the removal of the cuffs, neckline and bottom banding may differ.

1. To remove the cuffs, collar and bottom banding from the sweatshirt, cut close to the stitching line. Save the banding because it might be used later in the design.

2. Use a straight edge to draw a straight line, evening out the bottom edge of the sweatshirt.

3. To locate the center front of the sweatshirt, match the shoulder seams and fold the sweatshirt in half lengthwise. You can use an iron to press a crisp fold.

4. Cut along the fold.

5. To remove the sleeves for vest-style designs, cut along the seam line on the shoulder. Set aside the sleeves because they may be used at a later time.

6. After removing the banding, it is wise to stay stitch all edges to stabilize and prevent stretching. Stitch a row approximately ¼" from the freshly cut edges. When stabilizing the neckline, start stitching at the shoulder seams and stitch toward the center front and center back.

the
basics

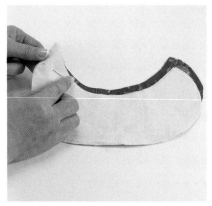

Apply interfacing to the collar pieces and pin the pieces right sides together.

Stitch the collar.

Press the collar.

Fold the ribbed binding over the stitching line.

Hand stitch the collar in place.

Collars

Fabric

1. Press interfacing to the wrong side of two collar pieces. With right sides together, pin the interfaced collars to the remaining collar sections.

2. Stitch the collar pieces together with ½" seam allowance.

3. Clip and trim the seams. Turn the piece right-side out and press.

4. Pin, then stitch the collar in place along the seam line where the binding meets the sweatshirt.

5. Fold the ribbed binding over the top of the stitching line, encasing the collar seam, and hand stitch in place.

Gently stretch the collar to fit the neckline.

Detail of the finished collar.

Knit A

1. Pin the knit collar to the inside of the neckline binding. Stitch with ¼" seam allowance.

2. Fold the collar to the front and press the knit collar on a low temperature.

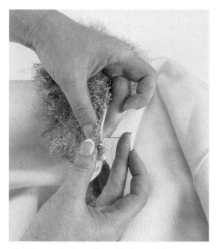

Gentrly stretch the collar to fit the neckline.

Detail of the finished collar.

Knit B

1. Pin the collar to the top edge of the ribbed neckline.

2. Using a needle and thread, sew the collar to the top of the ribbed banding using small stitches.

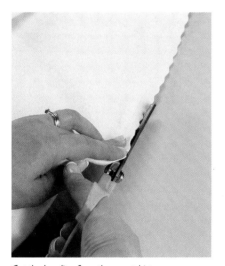

Cut the banding from the sweatshirt.

Stitch the ends of the collar.

Pin the banding along the neckline.

Ribbed binding

1. Cut the bottom banding from the sweatshirt.

2. Measure the circumference of the neckline edge. Use this measurement to cut a section of the bottom banding and add 1".

3. Turn the banding inside out and stitch the ends closed. Turn it right-side out and press.

4. Pin the banding along the neckline, gently stretching the binding to fit around the neckline. Stitch with ¼" seam allowance. Finish the edge with a satin stitch.

5. Sew lace trim along the bottom edge of the collar, finishing the ends by turning them under ½".

Adjust the length of the button loops to fit the buttons.

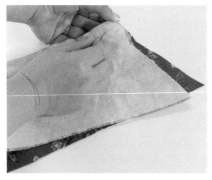

Pin the cuffs right sides together.

Stitch the cuffs together.

Press the cuffs.

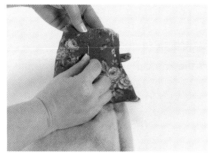

Pin the fabric cuff to the ribbed cuff.

Fold the fabric cuff over the ribbed cuff.

Cuffs

Fabric

1. Pin the button loops in place on the right side at the point marked on the pattern.

2. Press interfacing to the wrong side of the two cuff pieces. With right sides together, pin the interfaced cufs to the remaining cuff pieces.

3. With right sides together, stitch the cuff pieces together with ½" seam.

4. Clip and trim the seams. Turn right sides out and press.

5. Finish the bottom edge with a zigzag stitch. Turn the sleeve inside out and pin the right side of the fabric cuff to the wrong side of the ribbed cuff, stretching to fit.

6. Stitch with ½" seam. Turn the sweatshirt right-side out and fold the fabric cuff over the top of the ribbed cuff. Stitch a button opposite the button loop.

Stitch the quilted cuff seams.

Finish the cuff edge with bias tape.

The finished cuff.

Quilted fabric

1. Fold the cuff right-sides together and pin along the seam line. Stitch with ½" seam. Finish the edges with a zigzag stitch. Press the seam open.

2. Encase the top of the cuff edge with the seam binding. Finish the bottom edge with a zigzag stitch.

3. Turn the cuff wrong sides out and slip it inside the ribbed cuff, stretching the ribbed cuff to fit. Pin. Stitch with ½" seam. Fold the quilted cuff to the right side, covering the ribbed cuff.

Pin the right side of the cuff to the inside of the sleeve

Roll the finished cuff to the right side.

Hint

Remember to allow for the stretching required to fit your hand through the cuff.

Knit A

1. Using yarn, hand stitch the cuff together at the short ends.
2. Turn the sleeve wrong-side out and insert the knit cuff up into the sleeve and pin.
3. Stitch together with ¼" seam allowance. Turn the sleeve right-side out and fold the knit cuff to the right side, covering the ribbed cuff.

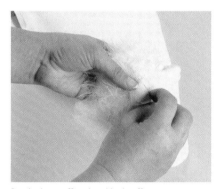

Pin the knit cuff to the ribbed cuff.

Sew the knit cuff on top of the ribbed cuff.

Knit B

1. Using yarn, hand stitch the knit cuff together along the short ends.
2. Pin the knit cuff to the right side of the ribbed cuff.
3. Using a needle and thread, hand stitch the cuff in place along the top and bottom edge.

Cuff pleat

1. Form a pleat on the outside lower edge of each sleeve by pinching together a 1" section of sleeve fabric along the bottom edge and pinning.
2. Secure the pleat with buttons, hand sewing through all layers of the sleeve fabric.

The finished cuff pleat.

getting started and finishing touches ❧ 15

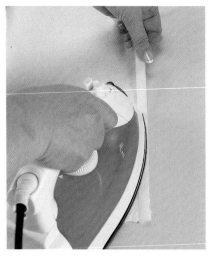

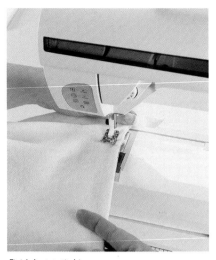

Lay the fusible web tape along the front opening.

Press the fusible web tape to the front opening.

Finish by topstitching.

Facings

Fusible web tape

1. Press fusible web tape along the front openings and bottom hem of the cardigan.
2. Remove the paper backing and turn under 1" along the front openings and bottom hem. Press.
3. Stitch close to the raw edges.

Fabric strip

1. Cut two strips of fabric 1½" wide x the length of the front sweatshirt opening, plus ½".
2. Fold under ¼" along one edge and press. Place the strip along the edge of the front opening of the sweatshirt right sides together and fold under ½" at the neckline.
3. Pin the facing onto the front opening on each side of the sweatshirt and stitch with ¼" seam.
4. Press to the underside of the sweatshirt. Stitch close to the folded edge.

Attach the front fabric strip facing.

Press the facing.

Sew the facing to the sweatshirt.

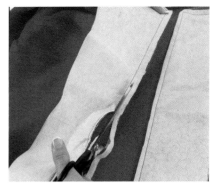

Clip the seams.

Turn the facing and press.

The finished facing.

Fabric facings (using two fabrics)

1. Press interfacing to the wrong side of the front and neck facing from Fabric A. Pin the front and neck facing from Fabric A together at the shoulder seam and stitch. Press the seams open.

2. Repeat stitching the facings together from Fabric B.

3. Pin the two facings (A and B) right sides together, matching the shoulder seams.

4. Place the sweatshirt on a flat surface and lay the facings on top. Baste through all layers, matching the front and neckline edges.

5. Stitch with ½" seam allowance.

6. Clip the seams close to the stitching line.

7. Turn and press, sandwiching the sweatshirt in between the facings. Press.

8. Finish the inside facing edge with a zigzag stitch. Press, then baste through all layers of the sweatshirt along the unfinished edge of the facing.

9. Starting at the bottom front edge of the sweatshirt, lay bias tape on top, covering the unfinished facing edge. Baste, then stitch close to both edges of the bias tape.

Stitch the facing to the sweatshirt.

Baste the edge of the facing.

Quilted fabric facings

1. Pin the facing along the front opening, wrong sides together. Stitch with ½" seam.

2. Fold the facing to the right side of the sweatshirt and press well. Press under ½" along the shoulder and side edges. Trim the fabric to fit close to the neckline edge.

3. Baste the edge of the facing along the front of the sweatshirt.

4. Stitch close to the neckline and along the shoulder and side edges of the facing. Turn the neckline ribbing over to cover the raw edges of the facing and hand stitch in place.

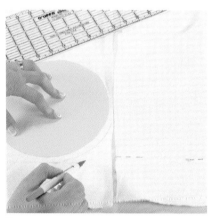
Trace the curve along the front of the sweatshirt.

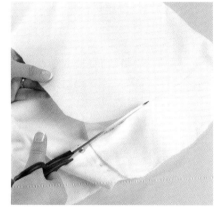
Cut along the traced lines.

Hemlines
Curved

1. Lay the sweatshirt on a flat surface and place a dinner plate or other round object on top of the sweatshirt, matching the front and bottom edges. Trace the curved line. Repeat for the opposite side.

2. Trim along these lines.

Measure and mark the angles.

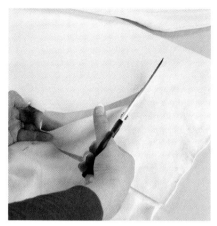

Cut along the traced lines.

Angular

1. Measure up 4" from the bottom edge of the sweatshirt and draw a line around the circumference of the sweatshirt.

2. Measure 4" from the front corner edge along the bottom hem and mark that point. Then measure 4" up along front edge (from the line you have already drawn). Draw a line connecting the two marks.

3. Cut along the marked lines.

Mark the scalloped edging.

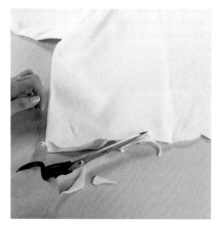

Trim the scalloped hemline.

Scalloped

1. To make the template, set a cup or other rounded object on top of a 3" sticky note pad.

2. Trace around the cup starting and finishing at the edge of the notepad.

3. Cut along this line.

4. Measure the circumference of the sweatshirt once the front edge has been hemmed. Divide that number by 3" (the width of the scallop). Any amount not divisible by three will add a small amount at a time to the scallops as you work around the sweatshirt. If when rounded, the number is an odd number, start at the front edged with a half scallop on each side.

5. Use a marking pen to mark scallops around the bottom of the sweatshirt. Cut along this line.

A selection of tea dyed doilies.

Carefully clip between stitches.

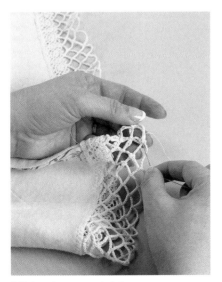

Fold the edges over and stitch.

Patterns

The patterns provided on the pattern sheet should be used with the knowledge that adjustments may be necessary. Sweatshirts are available from a variety of manufacturers and each is slightly different. When using facing patterns in particular, lay the pattern over the sweatshirt and check for any differences in the neckline, shoulder or length. Adjust by tracing directly onto the pattern, around the neckline and shoulder areas of the sweatshirt, adding or subtracting from the pattern as necessary.

Working With Vintage Linens and Crocheted Items

When looking for vintage linens, consider a couple of things prior to your purchase. The price should reflect the condition of the item as well as its age and uniqueness. Take a few minutes to check out the item, looking at the stitches and edge finishes. Take into account the size of the piece you will need for a project as well as the care required to clean the item. There are no guarantees as to the fiber content when purchasing items at thrift stores. Just be aware that you might not have what you think. Clean all purchased items prior to storing them. Gently soaking them in a mild solution of detergent and warm water is a good start. If the garment that the fabric will be attached to is to be machine-washed, test your purchased finds by washing them in the same manner as the finished garment will be washed. Remember that even a gently stained item can be restored by tea dyeing or selecting only the undamaged section for use.

Tea dyeing

Tea dyeing provides a sheer wash of color to items, giving them an antique look. To tea dye an item, fill a large pot with water and bring it to a boil. Add five tea bags and let them steep for 10 minutes. Add the fabric or doily to the pot and let it soak for five minutes. Remove. If you are happy with the color, rinse it under cold water, wring it out, and let it air dry. Press with a warm iron to set the color. If you want a darker color, return the item to the pot for an additional five minutes, continuing until you achieve your desired color.

Removing stitches

When using crocheted items attached to fabric, use a stitch ripper or small, sharp scissors to clip the stitches along the fabric edge, freeing the crocheted edge.

Finishing edges

Use small stitches and pearl cotton to secure the ends when cutting apart crocheted items. Add a drop of fabric glue to secure loose threads. Choose a location on the crocheted item that will cause the least amount of damage to the item. Cut around intricate crocheted motifs, folding threads behind the motif, and securing with stitches and glue.

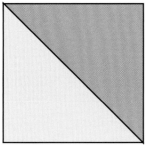
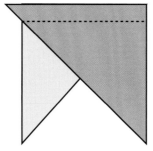
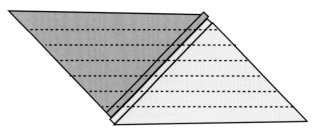

Fold the triangle in half diagonally. *Stitch with ¼" seam.* *Match the raw edges, stitch and press the seams open.*

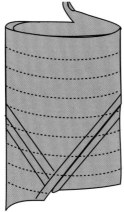
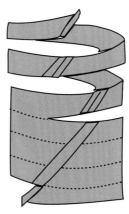

Match the lines, pin together and stitch. *Cut in a continuous line.*

Continuous Bias Binding

1. Cut a 27" square of binding fabric. Fold the square in half diagonally. Cut along the fold to make two triangles.

2. With right sides together and using ¼" seam allowance, machine stitch the triangles together. Press the seam allowances open.

3. On the wrong side of the fabric, draw two lines 2" apart, parallel to the long edges. Trim any fabric less than 2".

4. With right sides together, match the raw edges where the first line of the top section meets the second line of the bottom section. Insert pins along the drawn lines. Stitch using ¼" seam. Press the seams open.

5. Cut a continuous strip by beginning at one end, cutting along the lines around the tube.

6. Using a bias tape maker and following the manufacturer's instructions, insert one end of the fabric strip through the bias tape maker. Pull the fabric strip gently through the opposite end of the bias tape maker, pressing the folds in place as you work.

Continuous Bias Ruffle

1. Follow Steps 1 and 2 in Continuous Bias Binding, above.

2. On the wrong side of the fabric, draw lines 3" apart, parallel to the long edges. Trim any fabric less than 3". Refer to the illustration in Step 3, above.

3. Follow Steps 4 and 5 in Continuous Bias Binding, above.

4. Press the fabric strips in half lengthwise. Sew the rows of gathering stitches ¼" and ⅜" away from the raw edge along the length of the binding.

the skills

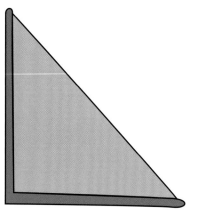

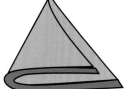

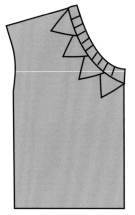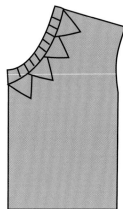

Fold the squares in half diagonally.   *Fold the triangle in half.*   *Pin in place along a neckline.*

Prairie Points

1. Cut 2" squares of fabric and fold them in half on the diagonal.

2. Fold each triangle in half again to create a prairie point.

3. Arrange the prairie points along the seam lines, overlapping as necessary to fit around the circumference of the sleeve and neckline. Pin, then stitch close to the raw edge.

knitting

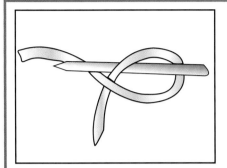

Drape the yarn over the needle.

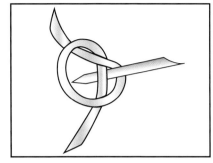

Pull the loop through.

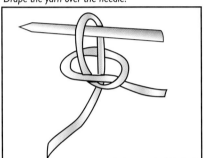

Tighten the knot underneath the needle.

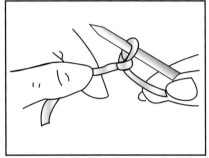

Slide the knot along the needle.

Slip knot

Make a loop on the needle and pull another loop through it. Tighten gently and slide the knot toward the needle.

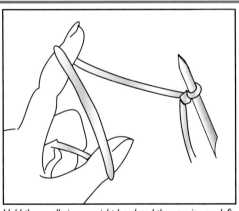

Hold the needle in your right hand and the yarn in your left.

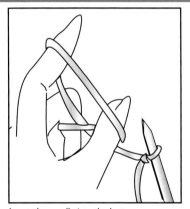

Insert the needle into the loop.

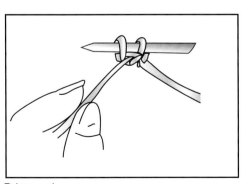

Tighten gently.

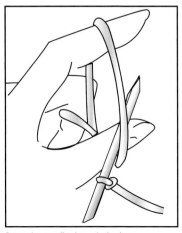

Bring the needle through the loop.

Casting on

Hold the needle with the slipknot in your right hand, the yarn going from the skein to your right hand. With your left hand, make a yarn loop. Insert the needle into the loop. Bring the needle through the loop and toward you, gently pulling the yarn end to make the loop snug, but not too tight. Repeat for each additional stitch. The slipknot counts as the first stitch.

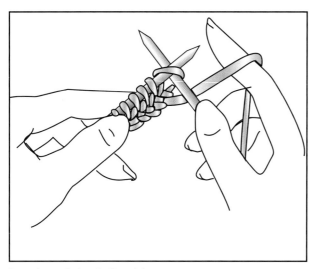

Insert the needle into the first stitch.

Wrap the yarn over the point of the right needle.

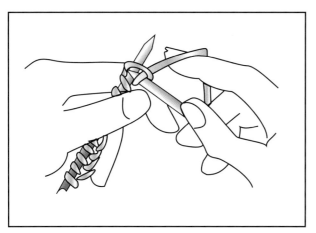

Pull the yarn through the stitch.

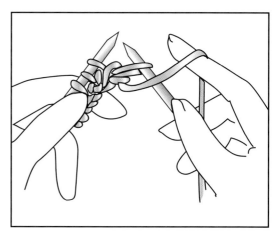

Slip stitch off the needle.

Knit stitch

Keeping the yarn behind the needles, insert the point of the right needle into the first stitch from the front to the back and under the left needle. With your right index finger, bring the yarn from the skein under and over the point of the right needle. Pull the yarn through the stitch with the right needle point. Slip the stitch off the left needle, leaving the new stitch on the right needle. Repeat to the end of the row.

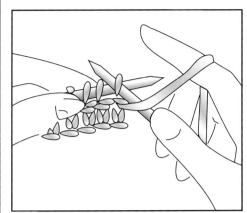

Insert the point of the right needle in front of the left needle.

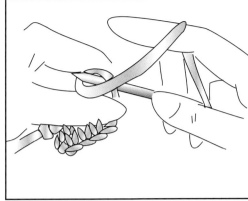

Wrap the yarn around the needle counterclockwise.

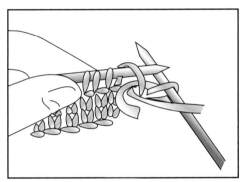

Draw the yarn back through the stitch.

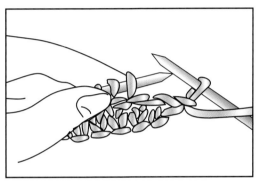

Slip stitch off the needle.

Purl stitch

Keeping the yarn in front of the needles, insert the point of the right needle into the first stitch from back to front and in front of the left needle. With your right index finger, bring the yarn from the skein around the right needle counterclockwise. Draw the yarn back through the stitch with the right needle point. Slip the stitch off the left needle, leaving the new stitch on the right needle. Repeat to the end of the row.

Knit one, purl one

Knit the first stitch, bringing the yarn between the needles toward the front. Purl the next stitch, bringing the yarn between the needle and toward the back. Continue to the end of the row.

Casting off

Knit the first two stitches. Insert the left needle into the first of the two stitches and pull it over the second stitch and completely off the needle. Knit one more stitch; insert the left needle into the first stitch on the right needle and pull the first stitch over the new stitch and completely off the needle. Continue to the end of the row. Draw the end of the yarn through the final stitch.

crocheting

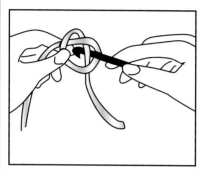

Make a loop on the hook.

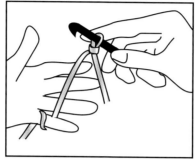

Slide the knot down the hook.

Slip knot

Make a loop on the hook and pull another loop through it. Tighten gently and slide the knot up to the hook.

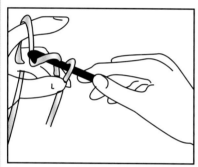

Wrap the yarn over the hook.

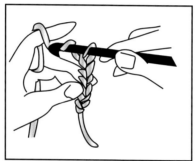

Slip the yarn through the loop of the hook.

Chain stitch

Start with a slip knot. Yarn over and slip the yarn through to form a new loop without tightening the previous loop. Repeat this to form the length of the chain desired. End by breaking the yarn and threading it trough the last loop.

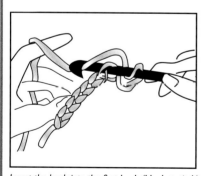

Insert the hook into the first hook (blanket stitch).

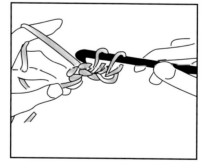

Wrap the yarn around the hook and pull it through both stitches (the blanket stitch counts as one stitch).

Single crochet

Crochetings will be attached to the sweatshirt by crocheting in to the blanket stitched eding along the sweatshirt hemlines, front, necklines and cuffs. Start with a slip knot. Insert the hook into the first blanket stitch, yarn over and slip the yarn back through the stitch only. Yarn over again and slip the yarn through both loops on the hook. The first single crochet is complete. Insert the hook into the second stitch and repeat.

Hint

If you desire a fuller look to crochet edging, single crochet into the same blanket stitch a second time.

embroidery stitches

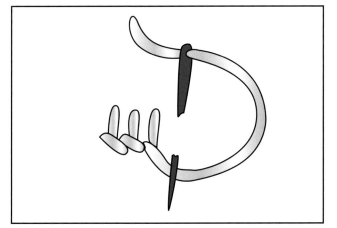

Blanket stitch.

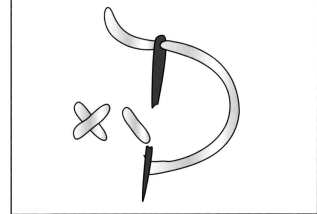

Cross stitch.

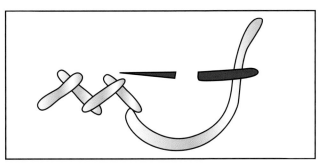

Herringbone stitch.

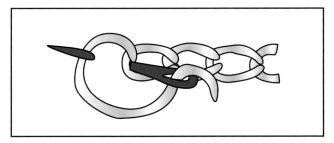

Chain stitch.

Redwork/back stitch.

Crazy patchwork quilting (a random assortment of fabric pieces) changed dramatically during the late 1800s with its popularity in Britain and America. The ornate style of the time turned the crazy quilt into a medium perfect for the displaying of needlework skills. A number of the designs in this book are embellished with crazy quilt embroidery. A few stitches can add just the right accent. Illustrations show how to execute the following stitches: redwork/back stitch, chain stitch, herringbone stitch, cross stitch and blanket stitch. Use either #8 pearl cotton or 6 ply embroidery floss for the embroidery stitches.

fashions with a purpose

Defy the ordinary by embellishing a basic wardrobe item into a distinctive, one-of-a-kind garment. Make the most of limited time by starting with a basic sweatshirt and utilizing simple techniques to apply yarns, embellishments and fabric accents. Make sewing fun with fast techniques that achieve a quality look without a lot of time.

periwinkle jacket

The periwinkle color
of the sweatshirt is a
blank canvas calling for
color. The bright colors in the
chenille/eyelash yarn are a
perfect accent.

Materials

- Periwinkle blue sweatshirt
- ½ yd. print fabric for the decorative shirt accents and purse
- ½ yd. solid fabric for the purse lining
- 1 skein (50 gram) of chenille and eyelash combination yarn*
- Fusible web tape (¼")
- ¼ yd. fusible web
- Bamboo purse handles
- Fabric marking pen
- Measuring tape/ruler
- Embroidery thread and needle
- Matching thread and needle
- Scissors
- Pins

* Used in this project: Patons Twister Yarn in Fruit Loops

Patterns
- Small kite

Cutting Instructions

Solid fabric
- Cut two squares 12" x 12" for the purse lining.

Print fabric
- Cut two squares 12" x 12" for the purse.
- Cut one piece 5½" x 3" for the pocket top.
- Cut one piece 7" x 5½" for the pocket.
- Cut one piece 1" x 8" for the pocket loop.
- Cut four pieces 2½" x 6" for the purse tabs.
- Cut one piece 1" x 6" for the back tab.
- Cut three kites, making sure to first apply fusible web to the wrong side of the fabric.

Instructions

1. Remove the banding from the bottom of the sweatshirt.
2. To make the front opening of the cardigan, lay the sweatshirt on a flat surface. Measure 1" away from the neckline binding along each shoulder seam and place a mark. Measure down 7" along the center front of shirt and place a mark. Draw a line from shoulder mark to the point at the center front on one side. Continue the curve from the 1" shoulder mark to the bottom of the neckline binding at the center back.
3. Cut along the lines.
4. Fold the sweatshirt to the opposite side and use your first curve as a pattern. Cut along the lines.
5. Stay stitch along the neckline edge.
6. To make the curved hemline, measure and mark a line 2" up from bottom hem. Cut along this line.
7. Using a dinner plate or other rounded object, draw a curve along the bottom front of the sweatshirt opening. Cut along this line (see page 18).
8. Press fusible web tape on the wrong side along the edge of the neckline and front and bottom hemline. Remove the paper backing and turn under ½" to the wrong side. Press well.
9. To make the pocket accents, cut two pieces 2" x 4" from the fabric removed from the bottom of the sweatshirt.
10. Fold the pieces in half lengthwise, right sides together, and press.
11. Stitch the short ends closed with ¼" seam. Turn the pieces right-side out and press.
12. Using the photograph as a guide, place the folded edge at an angle on each side of the shirt.
13. Topstitch the sides and bottom raw edge through all layers. Trim close to the stitching along the bottom edge.
14. To make the sleeve pocket, press fusible web tape to all edges of the 7" x 5½" print fabric.

Detail of the front pocket placement.

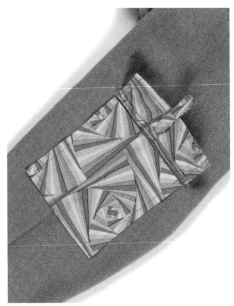

Detail of the sleeve pocket.

Back tab placement.

15. Remove the paper backing from the fusible web tape and turn the top edge of the pocket under ½" to the wrong side. Press the remaining three sides ½" to the wrong side.

16. Topstitch along the top of the pocket.

17. Center the pocket on the sleeve halfway between the cuff and the shoulder. Stitch it in place with ¼" seam along the sides and bottom.

18. To make the pocket top, fold the 1" x 8" print fabic for the pocket loop right sides together lengthwise and stitch with ¼" seam. Turn it right-side out and press.

19. Topstitch close to the edges.

20. Press fusible web tape along the 5½" sides of the pocket fabric.

21. Remove the paper backing and press under ½" to the wrong side.

22. Fold the pocket top in half, right sides out, and press.

23. Topstitch along the sides and folded edge of the pocket ¼" from the edge.

24. Wrap the pocket loop around the pocket top and pin at the center point, allowing the excess loop to hang below the folded edge of the pocket top.

25. Stitch the pocket loop to the pocket top.

26. Press the unfinished edge of the pocket top ¼" to the wrong side.

27. Pin the pocket top ¼" above the pocket and stitch along the top edge.

28. Remove the paper backing on the kite appliqués and fuse them on the back of the sweatshirt, below the neckline.

29. To create the pleat, measure 6" up from the bottom hem along the center back of the sweatshirt. Place a pin.

30. Measure 1" out from the first pin marking toward the side seams on each side and mark with pins.

31. Fold the two outside pins toward the middle pin to create an inverted pleat.

32. Using a needle and thread, stitch to secure the pleat. Remove the paper backing from the back tab and center it over the pleat. Press well.

33. Using embroidery thread, blanket stitch along the neckline, front hemlines, faux pocket edges, back tab and decorative designs on the back of the shirt (see page 27).

34. Single crochet two rows along the neckline, front hemline and faux pocket edges (see page 26).

35. Mark the placement, then sew four buttonholes to the right side of the sweatshirt.

36. Sew the buttons in place on the opposite side, matching the buttonholes.

37. Sew additional buttons to the left shoulder area and on the button loop on the arm pocket.

purse

1. Place the two 12" squares of print fabric on a flat surface. Measure and place a pin 2" in from the bottom on each side.

2. Place a ruler from the top edge to the 2" marking and draw a line. Trim along the marked line.

3. Fold over ½" to the wrong side at the top edge of each piece of fabric.

4. Starting with the print fabric, lay the pieces right sides together. Match the seams and stitch the side and bottom edges. Repeat with the lining fabric.

5. Turn and press.

6. With wrong sides together, match the seams and pin the lining to the inside of the bag.

7. Using the purse handles as a guide, measure 3½" down from the top edge and mark placement for the purse handles.

8. Fold each of the purse tabs in half lengthwise, right sides together, and stitch with ¼" seam. Turn right-side out and press.

9. Sew the tabs in place through both layers of fabric. Topstitch through both layers along the top edge of purse fabric.

10. Fold the cuff of the purse over and topstitch through both layers of fabric along the top edge to secure.

cropped
sunset

The color of a glorious
sunset teams with yarn
speckled with the colors of the
rainbow. The natural tones of the
buttons and purse handles work
to finish the design.

Materials

- Orange sweatshirt
- 1 skein (50 gram) worsted weight yarn*
- Fusible web tape (¼")
- Bell shaped purse handles
- Five buttons (½")
- Matching thread and needle
- Embroidery thread and needle
- Fabric marking pen
- Measuring tape/ruler
- Pins
- Scissors
- Crochet hook, size I/9

* Used in this project: Red Heart Hokey Pokey Yarn in 108 Tangerine

Instructions:

1. Remove the banding from the bottom of the sweatshirt.

2. To make the cardigan, lay the sweatshirt on a flat surface and measure 1" from the neckline binding along each shoulder seam and place a mark. Measure 4" down the center front of the shirt and mark. Draw a curved line from the shoulder mark to the point at the center front. Continue the curve from the 1" shoulder mark to the bottom of the neckline binding at the center back.

3. Cut along the lines.

4. Fold the sweatshirt over to the opposite side and use your first curve as a pattern. Cut along the lines.

5. Stay stitch along the neckline edge.

6. To make the hemline, measure and mark a line 4" up from the bottom hem. Cut along this line.

7. Measure and mark a line 16" up from each cuff edge. Cut the sleeves off at this line.

8. Press fusible web tape to the wrong side along the neckline, front, bottom hemline and sleeves. Remove the paper backing, turn under ½" to the wrong side and press well.

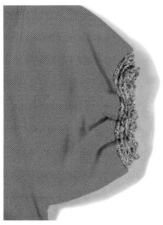

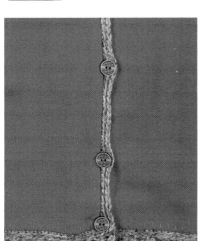

Crochet edging.

Crocheting

Review the crochet stitches on page 26.

Sleeves

Row 1 and 2: Single crochet into each blanket stitch around the sleeve.

Row 3: Decrease by single crocheting into every second loop, pulling the yarn taught as you work around the sleeve.

Decorative Edging

Row 4: Chain 4 stitches and single crochet in every second loop. Repeat around the circumference of the sleeve.

Cardigan

Row 1: Single crochet into each blanket stitch along the neckline, front and hemline. Create buttonholes on the right side of the sweatshirt by chaining two stitches, skipping two blanket stitches and continuing with the single crochet into each blanket stitch.

Row 2: Single crochet into each loop, working two single crochet stitches over each chain of two stitches.

Decorative Edging

Row 3: Use this along the bottom edge only. Chain four and single crochet in every second loop.

Bow

Crochet a 16" chain of stitches. Tie off and form a two-loop bow. Attach the bow to the pleat on the back of the shirt.

9. Using embroidery thread, blanket stitch along all edges at ¼" intervals (see page 27).

10. Mark the buttonhole placement with pins on the right side of the sweatshirt.

11. To make the pleat, mark the center back of the sweatshirt along the bottom hem with a pin.

12. Measure 2" out from the pin on each side and place a second and third pin on each side.

13. Fold the second and third pins toward the center pin to create an inverted pleat. Move the pins to secure the pleat.

14. When crocheting, line up the blanket stitches and treat them as one to hold the pleat in place.

15. Stitch the buttons to the left side of the sweatshirt opposite the buttonholes.

purse

1. Cut a straight line along the top of the leftover sleeve fabric to even the top edge.

2. Measure down 8" from that line and cut.

3. Turn it wrong-side out and stitch the narrow end closed.

4. Turn it right-side out and press.

5. Press the fusible web tape on the top edge of the purse. Remove the paper backing, turn under ½" and press.

6. Single crochet two strips, 4 rows x 24" long (see page 26).

7. Fold the crochet strips over 3" on each end and pin.

8. Pin the strip starting at the front top edge with the 3" section extending beyond the top edge of the purse and crossing over to the opposite side, around the back of the purse, and end by pinning to the opposite edge.

9. Stitch in place along both edges of the crochet trim. Repeat with the second strip.

10. The purse handles will slide through the loops.

11. Crochet a 20" chain of stitches for the bow (see page 26). Tie a bow and secure it to the front of the purse.

12. Crochet a 5" chain of stitches (see page 26). Fold it in half and attach it to the back of the purse.

13. Sew a button to the front of the purse.

mosaic tea party

My mother and I would enjoy an afternoon cup of tea together as I was growing up. The popularity of mosaics utilizing broken china and the memory of our afternoon teas was the inspiration for this design.

Materials

- Ivory sweatshirt
- ¼ yd. floral print fabric
- ¼ yd. fusible web
- Crocheted doilies
- 2½ yd. crochet style flat trim, 1" wide
- Ivory pearl cotton
- Embroidery needle
- Decorative teapot and spoon closures
- Non-stick ironing sheet
- Needle and thread
- Pins
- Scissors

Patterns

- Teapot
- Cup
- Saucer

Cutting Instructions

Floral print fabric
- Cut two strips 1½" x the length of the front sweatshirt opening plus ½".
- Cut several mosaic shapes, making sure to first apply fusible web to the wrong side of the fabric and remove the paper backing.

Instructions

1. Remove the banding from the bottom and neckline of the sweatshirt.
2. Cut down the center of the sweatshirt front to create a cardigan (see page 11).
3. Stay stitch along the neckline edge.
4. To make the collar, measure the circumference of the neckline edge.
5. Using the bottom banding with the stitching removed, cut a section that length plus 1".
6. Turn the banding inside out and stitch the ends closed. Turn right-side out and press.
7. Pin the banding collar along the neckline and stitch with ¼" seam.
8. Finish the edge of the collar with the satin stitch on your sewing machine.
9. Sew the lace trim along the bottom edge of the collar. Finish by turning the ends under ½".
10. To make the fabric facing, use the two strips of fabric 1½" wide x the length of the front sweatshirt opening plus ½". Fold the strips under ¼" along one edge and press (see page 16).
11. With right sides together, fold under ½" at the neckline and pin the facing onto the front opening on each side of the sweatshirt.
12. Stitch with ¼" seam. Press to the underside of the sweatshirt.
13. Stitch close to the folded edge on the underside of the sweatshirt.
14. Trace the teapot, cup and saucer patterns onto a piece of fusible web.
15. Remove one side of the paper backing and lay the fusible web, sticky-side up, on top of a non-stick sheet.
16. Lay the mosaic fabric pieces in place over the teapot, cup and saucer patterns that you traced onto fusible web, letting the pieces extend over the pattern. Allow ⅛" space between mosaics, cutting pieces to fit, if necessary.
17. When complete, fold the non-stick sheet over the top of the completed piece and press well. Let cool and peel off the sheet. Trim along the pattern lines.

Fill the pattern area with mosaic fabric pieces.

Press the area with a non-stick sheet over the appliqué.

Trim along the pattern lines.

18. Press the mosaic appliqués onto the sweatshirt using the non-stick sheet over the top to prevent excess from sticking to the iron.

19. Using the satin stitch setting on your sewing machine, stitch around each appliqué piece, finishing all raw edges.

20. Stitch the doily along the bottom hem of the sweatshirt. Repeat with a row of crochet trim. Wrap the excess around the front edges and stitch (see page 20).

21. Sew decorative closures to the front of the sweatshirt.

Embellish with a vintage doily.

I shall wear red and purple

Life can lead us along many paths and how we choose to travel can make all the difference in the world. Women around the country have joined hearts and hands to celebrate life at 50, all while proudly wearing the signature colors of red and purple as a badge.

Materials

- Red sweatshirt
- ¾ yd. floral print fabric
- ¾ yd. dark print fabric
- ¾ yd. light print fabric
- ¼ yd. lightweight fusible interfacing
- Two ½" buttons
- Matching thread and needle
- Scissors
- Pins

Patterns

- Front Facing
- Back Neck Facing
- Pocket
- Cuff

Cutting Instructions

Floral print fabric
- Cut two front facings.
- Cut two back neck facings.
- Cut two pockets.
- Cut two cuffs.

Dark print fabric
- Cut two front facings.
- Cut two back neck facings.
- Cut two pockets.
- Cut two cuffs.

Lightweight fusible interfacing
- Cut two front facings.
- Cut two back neck facings.

Light print fabric
- Create the continuous bias binding with the light print fabric (see page 21).

Instructions

1. Remove the banding from the collar and bottom of the sweatshirt.
2. Cut down the center of the sweatshirt front to create a cardigan (see page 11).
3. To make the facings, pin the floral print front and neck facings right sides together at the shoulder seam and stitch. Press the seams open. Repeat with the dark print facings.
4. Pin the dark print and floral print facings right sides together, matching the shoulder seams.
5. Place the sweatshirt on a flat surface, right-side out, and lay the facings on top.
6. Baste through all of the layers, matching the front and neckline edges.
7. Stitch through all of the layers. Clip the seams close to the stitching. Turn right-side out and press, sandwiching the sweatshirt in between the facings (see page 17).
8. Finish the inside facing edge with a zigzag stitch.
9. Press and pin the outside edge of the facings in place.
10. Pin the pocket sections right sides together.
11. Using the bias binding, finish the top edges of both pockets.
12. Position the pockets in place by tucking them under the front facing ½". Pin them in place.
13. Stitch along the lines marked on the pattern piece to create pockets.
14. Pin the bias binding on top of the raw edges of the front facing. Baste, then topstitch along both edges of the bias binding. Remove the basting stitches.
15. Fold the end of the bias binding at a 45-degree angle and press.
16. Starting at the bottom facing edge, sandwich the sweatshirt and pocket edge in the binding, ending with another 45-degree angle. Pin and baste.
17. Sew two rows of stitching along the binding.
18. Fold a 6" section of bias binding in half lengthwise and topstitch to create the fabric binding button loops. Cut the piece in half to make two button loops.
19. To make the cuffs, press interfacing to the wrong side of two cuff pieces.
20. With right sides together, insert the button loops, folded in half, inside the seam at the point marked, adjusting the length of the loop to match the size of button used. Pin in place.
21. Stitch the cuffs together. Clip and trim the seams. Turn the cuffs right-side out and press.
22. Finish the bottom edge of the fabric cuffs using a zigzag stitch.
23. Turn the sweatshirt inside out and stitch the fabric cuff in place at the seam line where the ribbed cuff meets the sweatshirt sleeve.
24. Turn the sweatshirt right-side out and fold the fabric cuff back over the knit cuff and sew the buttons in place.

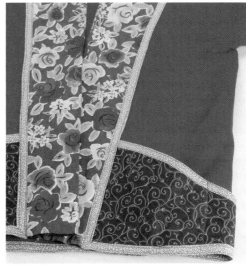

Finish the raw edges of the facing with the bias binding.

golden swirls

This design is formed around the yarn. The colors and textures bring this classy jacket to life. Wear it in good health and with much fun.

Materials

- Yellow sweatshirt
- ½ yd. print fabric for the swirl appliqué
- ½ yd. fusible web
- 1 skein (50 gram) multicolor eyelash yarn*
- Crochet hook, size G/6
- Knitting needles, size 10
- Variegated gold embroidery thread
- Embroidery needle
- Hook and eye
- 4 cover buttons (½")
- Matching thread and needle
- Pins
- Scissors

* Used in this project: Patons Cha Cha Yarn in Salsa

Patterns

- Swirl

Cutting Instructions

Print fabric

- Apply the fusible web to the wrong side of the print fabric. Trace and cut out the swirl appliqués (I used 16 swirl appliqués in my design).

Instructions

1. Remove the banding from the bottom and cuffs only.
2. Cut down the center of the sweatshirt front to create a cardigan (see page 11).
3. To make the curved hemline, lay the sweatshirt on a flat surface and place a dinner plate or other round object on top of the sweatshirt, matching the front and bottom edges. Trace a line. Repeat for the opposite side and trim along this line (see page 18).
4. Press under ½" along the front, bottom of the sleeves and hem.
5. Using the embroidery thread, sew a blanket stitch at ¼" intervals along the front edges, bottom of the sleeves and along the hem (see page 27).
6. Single crochet one row along the front and bottom hemlines (see page 26).
7. Knit a collar, using 70 stitches x 10 rows (see page 23).
8. Using matching thread, sew the collar to the top of the ribbed neck banding (see page 13).
9. Remove the paper backing from the swirl appliqués and fuse them in place on the front of the sweatshirt.
10. Using embroidery floss, sew a decorative running stitch around all of the designs.
11. Following the manufacturer's instructions, cover the buttons with the print fabric.
12. Form a pleat on the lower edge of each sleeve (see page 15). Secure each pleat with two buttons, hand sewing through all of the layers.
13. Stitch a hook and eye at top of the neckline.

Press the appliqués on the front of the sweatshirt.

Finish with a running stitch around the appliqués.

watercolor jacket

This jacket is perfect for planting your garden on a cool spring morning or for chasing the chill as the fall weather nears. Stay warm under a layer of floral flannel squares sewn together into the look of a watercolor quilt.

Materials

- Sage sweatshirt
- 1 yd. large floral print fabric (A)
- 1 yd. dark print fabric (B)
- ½ yd. floral print fabric (C)
- ½ yd. additional floral print fabric (D)
- ¼ yd. ivory washable felt
- ½ yd. fusible interfacing
- 1 package of 2" fusible nonwoven layout grid*
- 2 buttons (½")
- Matching thread and needle
- Pins
- Scissors
- Rotary cutter, ruler and mat

* Used in this project: 2" Quilt Press

Patterns

- Collar
- Cuff

Cutting Instructions

Large floral print fabric (A)
- Cut two collars.
- Cut four cuffs.
- Create a continuous bias binding (see page 21).
- Cut 2" squares according to the calculations in Steps 3-4.

Dark print fabric (B)
- Cut 2" squares according to the calculations in Steps 3-4.

Floral print fabric (C)
- Cut two collars.
- Cut 2" squares according to the calculations in Steps 3-4.

Floral print fabric (D)
- Cut 2" squares according to the calculations in Steps 3-4.

Fusible interfacing
- Cut two collars.
- Cut two cuffs.

Instructions

1. Remove the banding from the bottom of the sweatshirt only.
2. Cut down the center of the sweatshirt front to create a cardigan (see page 11).
3. Measure the bottom of the sweatshirt. Using this measurement, divide by 1½. Round the number up. The sweatshirt design shown utilizes this number of squares x 6.
4. Following the fusible nonwoven grid manufacturer's instructions, use a rotary cutter, ruler and mat to cut 2" squares of each fabric. Cut more than the actual number to allow for design changes.
5. Arrange the 2" squares on the fusible nonwoven layout grid to create the design.
6. Press the squares onto the grid and stitch, following the manufacturer's instructions.
7. Press under ¼" along the top edge of the completed watercolor piece.
8. Center the design along the bottom edge of the sweatshirt and pin. Trim the excess along the front edges.

Lay the fabric squares on the fusible grid.

Sew the finished watercolor section to the sweatshirt.

9. Baste the piece in place along the top, front and bottom edge. Topstitch along the top edge of the watercolor piece.

10. Press the fusible web to the back of the felt.

11. Cut two 1" and two 1½" strips of felt.

12. Place the 1" strips parallel to the bottom edge at 3" and 6" intervals. Press, then stitch in place.

13. Cut five 9" lengths from the 1½" strips of felt. Cut a point at the top of each length to create fence posts.

14. Set the fence posts in place on top of the horizontal strips, starting at the center back, spacing the posts evenly around the sweatshirt.

15. Press and stitch.

16. To make the collar, press interfacing to the wrong side of two collar pieces.

17. Pin the interfaced collar pieces to the remaining collar pieces right sides together and stitch with ¼" seam. Clip and trim the seams. Turn the collar right-side out and press.

18. Pin, then stitch the collar in place along the seam line where the binding meets the sweatshirt.

19. Fold the ribbed binding over the top of the stitching line, encasing the collar seam, and hand stitch it in place.

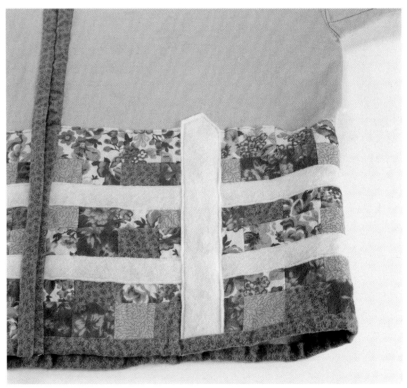

Detail of the fence post trim.

20. Using the bias binding from the large floral print fabric (A), encase the front and bottom hem of the jacket. Baste and stitch.

21. Fold a 6" section of bias binding in half lengthwise and topstitch to create the fabric binding for the button loops. Cut in half.

22. To make the cuffs, press the interfacing to the wrong side of the two cuff pieces.

23. With right sides together, insert the button loops, folded in half, inside the seam at the point marked, adjusting the length of the loop to match the size of the button used. Pin them in place.

24. Stitch the cuffs together. Clip and trim the seams. Turn the cuffs right-side out and press.

25. Sew a zigzag stitch along the unfinished edge of the fabric cuffs.

26. Turn the sweatshirt inside out and stitch the fabric cuff in place at the seam line where the ribbed cuff meets the sweatshirt sleeve.

27. Turn the sweatshirt right-side out and fold the fabric cuff back over the knit cuff.

28. Sew the buttons in place.

photo

and lace

The techniques of transferring photographs to fabric are varied, each offering a different feel or ease of use. If you are not adept at crocheting, use wonderful vintage doilies to frame your photograph.

Materials

- Ivory sweatshirt
- 1 sheet of photo transfer fabric*
- Crocheted doilies
- Lace appliqué (optional)
- Fusible web tape (½")
- Ivory pearl cotton, size 8
- Embroidery needle
- Decorative buttons
- Wax paper
- Matching thread and needle
- Pins
- Scissors
- Scalloped or pinking shears
- Thin cardboard
- Fabric glue*

* Used in this project: Avery Printable Fabric and Fabri-Tac

Detail of the blanket stitch trim.

Trim around the photo.

Attach the photo to the lace appliqué.

Instructions

1. Remove the banding from the bottom of the sweatshirt.
2. Cut down the center of the sweatshirt front to create a cardigan (see page 11).
3. Press the fusible web tape along the wrong side of the front and bottom edges.
4. Using scalloped scissors, trim close to the edges.
5. Remove the paper backing. Turn under ½" along the bottom hem and press well.
6. Turn under 1" along the front opening and press.
7. Remove the center fabric from the doily, being careful not to cut into the stitching (see page 20). Pin the doily along the top edge of the neck binding, adjusting the length of the doily by gathering slightly or trimming to fit.
8. Using the ivory pearl cotton, blanket stitch at ⅛" intervals along the top edge of the ribbed neck binding and doily (see page 27).
9. Using the ivory pearl cotton and starting at the bottom front of the sweatshirt, sew a blanket stitch at ¼" intervals (see page 27). Create a scallop by stitching 1½" up into the sweatshirt on every 16th stitch. Reinforce with a couple of stitches and continue working around the sweatshirt. Work from each side, adjusting the amount of stitches to meet in the back. Repeat this step for cuff edges, stitching up into the cuff every six stitches.
10. Following the manufacturer's instructions, create a photo transfer on muslin fabric. Cut out an oval cardboard shape to fit your photo. Center the cardboard over the photo. Draw a line ¼" from the cardboard edge along the fabric. Cut along this line.
11. With the right side of the photo down, center the cardboard over the photo and cut slits into the fabric close to cardboard edge. Do not cut into the cardboard. Press the fabric over the cardboard, overlapping the edges of the fabric as you work around the oval.
12. Remove the cardboard, and using the ivory pearl cotton, sew a blanket stitch at ⅛" intervals around the circumference of the photo (see page 27).
13. Center the photo over the lace appliqué and either glue in place or blanket stitch the photo on top of the lace (see page 27).
14. Glue the lace accent in place on the left front of the sweatshirt. Due to the sheer nature of lace, be careful not to apply too much glue.
15. Sew decorative buttons to the front of the sweatshirt.

Hint

A crocheted doily may be substituted for lace appliqué. Glue the center first, then carefully lift the lace. Using a paintbrush or toothpick, apply glue as you work toward the outside edge. Place a piece of waxed paper on top of the design and a heavy object on top of the waxed paper. Set aside to dry.

bed jacket

The lady of the house never looked better with generous bell shaped sleeves and long flowing ties draping down from the neckline. Soft pastel fabric insets turn a plain sweatshirt into something almost decadent.

Materials

- Pink sweatshirt
- 1 yd. satin-backed flannel
- ¼ yd. lightweight fusible interfacing
- Matching thread and needle
- Scissors

Patterns

- Collar
- Sleeve Inset

Cutting Instructions

Satin-backed flannel

- Cut two sleeve insets.
- Cut four collars.
- Create a continuous bias binding (see page 21).

Lightweight fusible interfacing

- Cut two collars.

Instructions

1. Remove the banding from the bottom of the sweatshirt.
2. Cut down the center of the sweatshirt front to create a cardigan (see page 11).
3. Cut each sleeve open along the seam line up to within ½" of the armhole.
4. With right sides together, set the sleeve insets in place, matching the seam lines and large dot to the pin marking.
5. Stitch the sleeve insets to the sweatshirt with ¼" seam, breaking the stitching at the dot, if necessary. Press the seams outward.
6. Finish the edges with a zigzag stitch.
7. To make the collar, press interfacing to the wrong side of two collar pieces.
8. Pin the interfaced collar pieces to the remaining collar pieces right sides together and stitch with ¼" seam. Turn the collar right-side out and press.
9. Pin and stitch the collar in place along the neckline at the point where the binding is sewn to the sweatshirt.
10. Fold the ribbed binding over the top of the stitching line, encasing the collar seam, and sew it in place.
11. Place a pin 6" from the bottom front corner at each side of the sweatshirt. Place pins at the center top of the neckline. Lay a strip of bias binding running between the two pins on each side. Baste in place. Stitch close to the edges of the binding strip along each side.

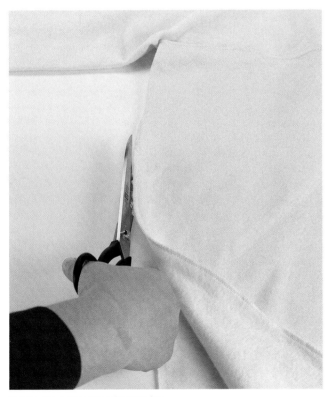

Cut the sleeve open along the seam line.

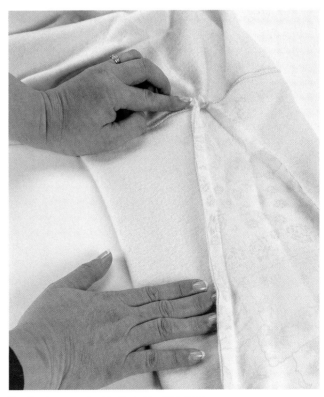

Sew the sleeve gore inset to the inside of the sleeve.

Encase the sleeve, hemline and front of the jacket with bias binding.

12. To make the curved hemline, lay a dinner plate or other round object on top of the sweatshirt, matching the front and bottom edges, and trace a line. Repeat for the other side and trim along this line (see page 18).

13. Using the bias binding, encase the bottom of the sleeves and front and bottom hem of the jacket. Baste and then stitch.

14. To make the decorative tie closure, fold two 32" lengths of bias tape lengthwise, right sides together. Stitch with ¼" seam. Turn inside out and press.

15. Form two loops at the top of each tie and stitch in place at the top of the neckline on each side or jacket. Tie a knot at the end of each tie.

on the town with style

These designs are suitable for a night on the town or as dressy daywear. Create jackets and vests with interesting silhouettes, dabs of color and complementary textured trims. Satin fabrics, innovative trims, elegant yarns, fur and beaded accents fill the pages in this chapter. Sweatshirts have never looked so elegant.

beaded
white
on white

Mohair yarn adds a touch
of class to this design.
The iron-on beads
are simple to use and
provide a designer look
when combined with the
mohair collar and cuffs and
stitched beaded trims.

Materials

- White sweatshirt
- 1 skein (50 gram) white mohair yarn*
- Clear iron-on beads with paper*
- Knitting needles, size 10
- White pearl cotton, size 8
- Matching thread and needle
- Hook and eye
- Pins
- Scissors
- Pencil

* Used in this project: Gedifra Tecno Hair Yarn, Beads-2-Fuse

Patterns

- Coil

Cutting Instructions

- Iron-on bead paper
- Cut 22 coil designs using the pattern.

Hint

To save time, use a paper punch or diecut machine to cut the swirl designs.

Instructions

1. Remove the banding from the bottom of the sweatshirt.
2. Cut down the center of the sweatshirt front to create a cardigan (see page 11).
3. Measure up 3" from the bottom edge and place pins lying horizontally around the circumference of the shirt. Mark the center back with a vertical pin.
4. To make the curved hemline, place the sweatshirt on a flat surface. Place a dinner plate or other round object on top of the sweatshirt, matching the front edge and the line of pins. Trace a line. Continue around the side of the sweatshirt, tracing along the pins. Draw a curve down toward the center back pin, ending in a point. Fold the sweatshirt in half and cut out both sides at once.
5. Turn under ½" hem along the front and bottom edges. Press well.
6. Finish the hem with a blanket stitch at ¼" intervals, adding a bead to every third stitch (see page 27).
7. Knit a collar and cuffs (see page 23).

   Collar: 70 stitches x 10 rows

   Cuffs: 40 stitches x 10 rows
8. Attach the collar to the top edge of the ribbed neckline with a needle and thread (see page 13).
9. Using the white mohair yarn, stitch the cuff seams together (see page 15). Pin the knit cuff on top of the ribbed cuff. Hand stitch in place along both edges.

Hint

Remember to allow for the stretching required to fit your hand into the cuff.

Complete the hemline with a blanket stitch.

10. Following the manufacturer's instructions, fuse the beads in place on top of the coil cutouts.

11. Stitch a hook and eye in place at the neckline edge.

Press decorative beads on the front of the sweatshirt.

fur-trimmed vest and purse

A friend of mine was proudly showcasing a vest she had just received as a gift. While the interpretation of the vest is mine, her confident attitude is what I truly wanted to capture.

Materials

- Black sweatshirt
- ½ yd. washable fur
- 1¼ yd. cording
- 22" separating zipper
- Black Velcro (1" wide)
- Fabric marker
- Matching thread and needle
- Measuring tape or ruler
- Pins
- Scissors

Cutting Instructions

- Measure and cut four strips of fur 3" wide.

Hint

When cutting fur, mark the cutting line, then cut along the fabric backing only.

Instructions

1. Remove the banding from the bottom of the sweatshirt.
2. Cut down the center of the sweatshirt front to create a cardigan (see page 11).
3. Remove the sleeves and an additional ½" around the inside of the armhole.
4. Measure the circumference of the armhole opening and cut a piece of fur this length plus 1".
5. Sew the ends of the fur together with ½" seam.
6. With right sides together, pin the fur along the armhole edge and sew with ½" seam.
7. Turn the fur to the inside and hand sew in place over the stitching line.
8. Measure the neckline along the banding at the seam line and cut a piece of fur 1" less than this measurement.
9. Pin the fur in place starting ½" in from the front edge along this seam line.
10. Stitch the fur in place close to the edge.

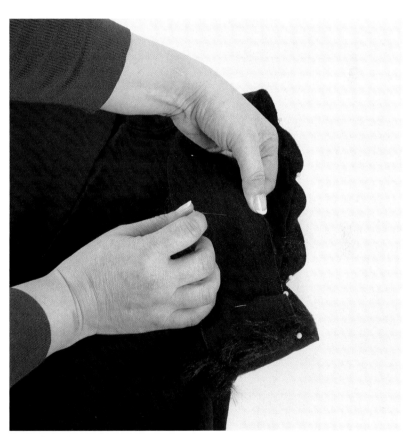

Pin the fur to the sleeve opening.

Pin the fur trim along the marked line at the bottom of the sweatshirt.

11. Turn the banding over the stitching line, enclosing the fur edge, and hand stitch in place.

12. Press under ½" along the front edges of the sweatshirt and baste.

13. Sew the zipper down the front of the sweatshirt. Hand stitch the zipper ends in place neatly at the neckline edge.

14. Measure and mark a line 2½" up from bottom edge of the sweatshirt.

15. With right sides together, pin fur above this line and stitch.

16. Turn the fur over the seam and and pin the matching bottom edge of the sweatshirt and fur.

17. Sew the sweatshirt and fur together with a close zigzag stitch.

18. Stitch the edges of the fur neatly along the zipper edge.

purse

1. Cut a straight line along the top of the leftover sleeve fabric to even the top edge.

2. Measure down 8" from that line and cut.

3. Turn it wrong-side out and stitch the narrow end closed.

4. Opening the seam, measure in 1" from each point and stitch across the bottom.

5. Turn it right-side out and press.

6. Measure the top circumference of the purse and cut a strip of fur 2" wide by the circumference, adding 1".

7. With right sides together, stitch the ends of the fur together.

8. Cut two 3" pieces of satin cording.

9. Fold the cording in half and pin, matching the raw edges of the loops along the seam on the inside of the purse at each side.

10. Pin the right side of the fur to the inside of the purse and stitch.

11. Turn the fur cuff to the outside and press the fabric carefully.

12. Thread the remaining length of cording through the loops and tie at each side.

Cut the fabric for the purse from the removed sleeve.

bolero

jacket

Simple lines and a funky trim stitched together create a fun bolero jacket. Choose warm neutral colors or jazz it up with hot jewel tones. Wear it over a simple dress or pair it with jeans and heels.

Materials

- Ivory sweatshirt
- 4 yd. brown hairy gimp trim
- 1 yd. beige hairy gimp trim
- Hook and eye
- Fabric marker
- Matching thread and needle
- Measuring tape or ruler
- Pins
- Scissors

Instructions

1. Remove the banding from the bottom and cuffs of the sweatshirt.

2. Cut down the center of the sweatshirt front to create a cardigan (see page 11).

3. To make the angular hemline, measure up 4" from the bottom edge around the circumference of the sweatshirt and cut off. Measure and mark 4" from front corner edge along the bottom hem and 4" up along the front edge. Draw a line connecting the two marks and cut along this line (see page 19).

4. Turn under ½" along the front, bottom and cuff edges to the right side. Press.

5. Fold the ribbed neckline banding toward the inside of the neckline edge, folding the ends under. Press and pin to secure.

6. Measure the circumference of the neckline and cut a section of beige gimp this length plus 1".

7. Fold the ends of the beige gimp trim under pin in place.

8. Stitch the gimp in place using a fine zigzag stitch along the neckline edge on top of the banding, which will act as the facing.

9. Fold the gimp trim back over the top of the stitching line and pin a row of brown gimp under the beige gimp.

Pin the beige gimp along the neckline.

Pin the brown gimp under the beige gimp.

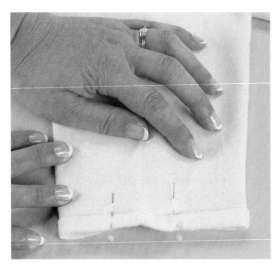

Mark the trim placement along the bottom of the sleeve.

10. Stitch the brown gimp in place.

11. Stitch the brown gimp in place along the front and bottom edges of the sweatshirt enclosing the ½" folded edge.

12. Locate the center front of the sleeve along the bottom edge by folding the sleeve in half and placing a mark opposite the seam. Measuring from the center bottom, place a mark 3" up from center mark and 1" on either side along the bottom edge.

13. Sew the brown hairy gimp in place on the sleeves starting at the underarm seam line, stitching to the first mark. Stop with the needle in the fabric and pivot, sewing the gimp up to the second mark. Stop, pivot once again, and continue down to the third mark. Pivot one last time and continue around the sleeve. Repeat for the second sleeve.

14. Roll the ½" seam that is left exposed on the front of the sleeve, enclosing the raw edge, and neatly stitch to hold it in place.

15. Stitch a hook and eye in place at the neckline edge.

Attach the gimp to the sleeve.

*black
fun
fur*

The knitted
fur collar
and daring
neckline make
this sweatshirt
pure fun. Match
the yarn to
the sweatshirt color
or spice it up with a
contrasting color.

Materials

- Black sweatshirt
- 1 skein (50 gram) black fun fur yarn*
- 1 package black extra wide bias binding
- 1¼ yd. black satin cording
- Knitting needles, size 10
- Matching thread and needle
- Measuring tape or ruler
- Fabric marking pen
- Pins
- Scissors

* Used in this project: Lion Brand Fun Fur

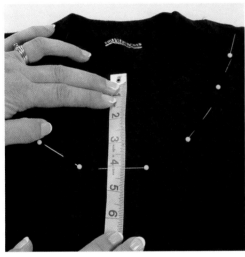

Mark the neckline of the sweatshirt.

Instructions

1. Remove the banding from the bottom and neckline of the sweatshirt. **Do not** cut down the front of this shirt.

2. On the center front of the sweatshirt, measure down 3" from the neckline edge and place a mark.

3. Place a mark 1" in from the neckline on the shoulder seam.

4. Draw a gently curved line connecting the marks on each side.

5. Stitch along this curved line. Cut the excess fabric close to the stitching line.

6. Cut a section of black bias binding the length of the circumference of the neckline plus 1".

7. With right sides together, sew the bias binding along the sweatshirt neckline, overlapping the ends. Stitch ¼" seam.

8. Fold the binding to the inside, pin in place and press.

9. Stitch along the bottom edge of the binding.

10. Knit a collar with the black fun fur yarn (see page 23).

    Collar: 140 stitches x 10 rows.

11. Attach the collar to the right side of the sweatshirt along the neckline, starting 4" left of the center (see page 13). Hand stitch in place.

12. Measure 10" up from the bottom of the ribbed cuff and around the circumference of the sleeve and cut off.

13. Measure the circumference of the bottom of the sleeve. Cut open one removed sleeve along its length. Measure and cut a 2" wide strip from the widest point along the top of the removed sleeve. Cut the 2" wide strip the length of the circumference of the bottom of the sleeve measured earlier, less 2". Sew the short ends together with ¼" seam.

14. Fold the 2" strip in half right sides out and stretch over the bottom of the sleeve, matching seams and pin. Stitch with ¼" seam. Finish the seam with a zigzag stitch. Repeat for the other side.

15. Cut two 12" lengths of satin cording.

16. Tie two two-loop bows and stitch them to the front of the cuffs.

17. Tie a two-loop bow with the remaining cording and attach it to the front of the sweatshirt.

18. Tie a knot 1" up from each cording end.

jazzy
chenille

The wonderful chenille yarn with color flecks match three of the fabric pieces perfectly. The covered buttons bring those bright colors to your attention and create a funky detail.

Materials

- Black sweatshirt
- ¼ yd. each of three complementary fabrics (A, B and C)
- Fusible web tape (½" wide)
- 1 skein (50 gram) chenille yarn*
- Knitting needles, size 10
- 5 cover buttons (½")
- Matching thread and needle
- Pins
- Scissors

* Used in this project: Chenille Thick & Quick Yarn in Kaleidoscope 203

Cutting Instructions

Fabric A
- Cut one 4" square.
- Cut one 4" x 10" rectangle.

Fabric B
- Cut one 4" square.
- Cut one 4" x 10" rectangle.

Fabric C
- Cut one 4" square.
- Cut one 4" x 10" rectangle.

Instructions

1. Remove the banding from the bottom of the sweatshirt.
2. Cut down the center of the sweatshirt front to create a cardigan (see page 11).
3. Press fusible web tape along the front opening and bottom hem.
4. Remove the paper backing from the fusible web tape and turn under 1" along the front opening and bottom hem. Press.
5. Topstitch the front opening and bottom hem close to the raw edges.
6. Knit a collar and cuffs (see page 23).

   Collar:

   70 stitches with a K1 – P1 pattern for 10 rows.

   Cuffs:

   40 stitches with a K1 – P1 pattern for 10 rows. Using yarn, stitch cuffs seams together.
7. To attach the cuff, insert the right side of the knit cuff into the sleeve, matching the edge of the knit cuff with the edge of the ribbed cuff (see page 15).
8. Stitch the cuffs with ¼" seam. Fold the knit cuff to the right side, covering the ribbed cuff.
9. To attach the collar, face the right side of the collar to the inside of the neckline banding. Stitch the collar with ¼" seam. Fold the collar over the neckline to the front of the sweatshirt and press (see page 12).
10. With right sides together, sew the three 4" x 10" rectangles together along the 10" lengths with ½" seam. Press the seams toward the outside edges.
11. Cut an 8" square, turning the square on point. Press fusible web tape along the raw edges on the right side of the fabric square.
12. Center the 8" square on the wrong side of the back of the sweatshirt.

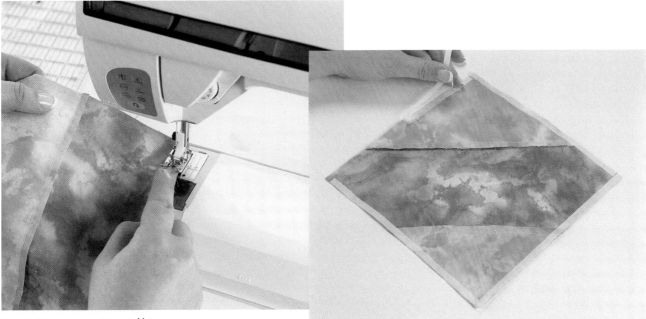

Sew the fabric strips together with ½" seam.

Press the fusible web tape to the right side of the fabric.

Detail of the stitching lines.

13. Remove the paper backing from the fusible web and press the square in place.

14. Stitch close to the raw edges around the square.

15. Turn the sweatshirt right-side out. Topstitch from top to bottom down the center from point to point, working your way to the opposite side with ½" seams.

16. Using sharp scissors, cut between each row of stitching.

17. Draw a line horizontally across the middle of the design. Sew a line of stitching over that line, finger pressing the fabric all one direction.

18. Mark the next two rows, 2" on either side, and repeat Step 17, reversing the directions of the fabric when stitching.

19. Mark the final two rows 1½" on either side of the second and third rows, once again reversing the direction of fabric before stitching.

20. The three remaining 4" squares will be applied and stitched in the same manner on the front of the sweatshirt. Line the squares point to point, down the front side of the shirt (see the photo for placement). Press in place and topstitch using the instructions in Steps 11 through 18.

21. Cover the five buttons with fabric following the manufacturer's instructions. Mark the placement, then sew the five buttonholes.

22. Sew the buttons in place to the opposite side of the front of the sweatshirt, matching buttonholes.

swing jacket

I have always liked the look of the classic swing-style jacket. The idea to insert panels into the sweatshirt came from a young girl's jeans. The wonderfully bright fabric insets changed her everyday jeans into a personal fashion statement.

Materials

- Red sweatshirt
- 1½ yd. floral print fabric
- Fusible web tape (¼" wide)
- 1½ yd. braided trim
- 1 decorative button
- Hook and eye closure
- Needle and thread
- Pins
- Scissors
- Measuring tape

Patterns

- Left Yoke
- Right Yoke
- Back Neck Facing
- Sleeve Inset
- Gore Inset

Cutting Instructions

Floral print fabric

- Cut two sleeve insets.
- Cut one left yoke.
- Cut one right yoke.
- Cut one back neck facing.
- Cut five gore insets.
- Create a continuous bias binding (see page 21).

Instructions

1. Remove the banding from the bottom, neckline and cuffs of the sweatshirt. Stay stitch along all edges.
2. Cut down the center of the sweatshirt front to create a cardigan (see page 11).
3. Fold the sweatshirt in half, matching the front openings and press a crease along the center back.
4. Match the center back line with the front opening and press a crease along the side seams.
5. Fold the front of the sweatshirt back so that the front openings match the side seams at each side and press a crease.
6. Measure up 14" along each pressed crease and cut.
7. Press a crease on the opposite side of the sleeve from the seam line. Measure up 14" along these pressed creases and cut.
8. Cut along the sleeve seam line, removing the stitching up to within 1" of the armhole. Place a pin ½" above each cut.
9. With right sides together, set the sleeve inset in place, matching the underarm seam lines and marking the dot on the pattern with a pin.
10. Stitch the insets with ¼" seam, breaking the stitching at the pin, if neccessary. Press the seams outward. Finish the edges with a zigzag stitch.
11. With right sides together, set the gore inset in place, matching the seam lines.
12. Stitch the insets with ¼" seam, breaking the stitching line at the pin, if necessary. Press the seams outward. Finish the edges with a zigzag stitch.
13. Stitch the right and left yoke to the back neck facing with ½" seams and press the seams open.
14. Press fusible web tape to the wrong side along the bottom edges of the right and left yoke and back neck facing.

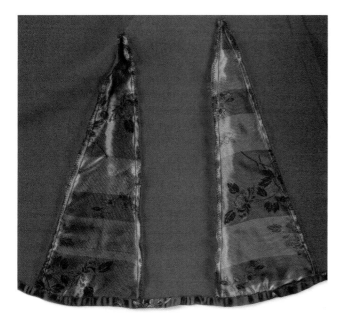

Detail of the completed gore insets (inside view).

15. Pin the right side of the facings to the wrong side of the sweatshirt, matching the shoulder seams and front edges.

16. Stitch the facings with ½" seam. Trim the seam and clip the curves. Turn and press.

17. Remove the paper from the fusible web tape and press the facings to the right side of the jacket.

18. Clip the front edge of the right and left yoke at the end of the facing and turn under ½" to create a finished edge along the front of the shirt.

19. Stitch the braided trim to cover all of the unfinished edges of the yoke facings.

20. Encase the bottom edges of the jacket and sleeves with the bias binding. Turn the bias binding ends under for a finished look.

21. Finish with a decorative button and a hook and eye closure at the neckline.

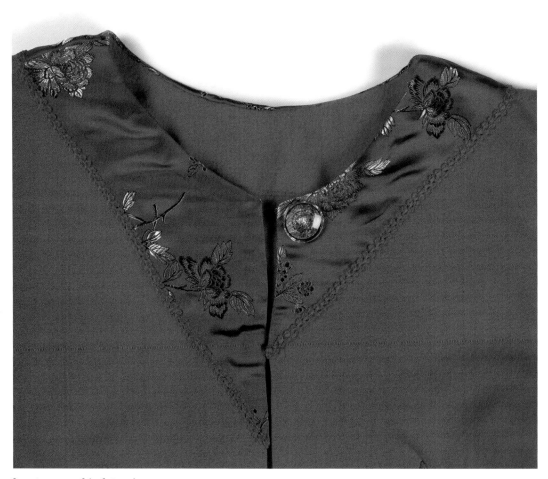

Sew trim on top of the facing edges.

everyday fashion fun

These designs utilize fun trims, innovative new products and basic embroidery stitches.

buttons and beads

The u-shaped neckline draws the eye down the front of the shirt to the bottom hem. Beaded trims add a casual, yet sophisticated, look.

Materials

- Black sweatshirt
- Fusible web tape (½" wide)
- 1½ yd. beaded trim
- 4 buttons (¾")
- Fabric marker
- Snap fastener
- Ruler
- Needle and thread
- Pins
- Scissors

Instructions

1. Remove the banding from the bottom of the sweatshirt.
2. Cut down the center of the sweatshirt front to create a cardigan (see page 11).
3. On the center front of the sweatshirt, measure down 4" from the neckline edge and place a mark.
4. Place a mark 1" out from neckline binding along the shoulder seam.
5. Draw a u-shaped curve from the shoulder mark to the point at the center front on one side. Continue the curve drawing a line from the shoulder mark to the bottom of the neckline binding at the center back.
6. Cut along this curved line. Fold to the opposite side and use as a pattern.
7. Stay stitch neckline edge.
8. To finish the neckline, trim the ribbed banding that was removed from the bottom edge to 2" wide.
9. Measure the neckline and subtract 4" from this measurement. Cut the banding the length of this measurement.
10. Turn the banding wrong-side out and stitch the ends closed.
11. Turn the banding right-side out and pin in place along the neckline on the right side of the sweatshirt.
12. Stitch using ¼" seam. Press. Finish with a zigzag stitch.

Measure and mark the neckline.

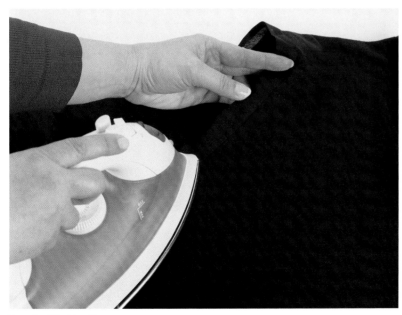

Press the ribbed banding.

Detail of the finished neckline banding.

Pin the cuff banding to the bottom of the sleeve.

13. Measure up 10" from the ribbed cuff and cut off that part of the sleeve.

14. Measure the bottom edge of the trimmed sleeve. Do not stretch. Subtract 2" from this measurement and cut a section of the 2" wide banding this length.

15. Fold the banding in half lengthwise and stitch the ends together.

16. Stretch the banding over the bottom of the sleeve and pin.

17. Stitch with ¼" seam. Press. Finish the seams.

18. Repeat steps 13 through 17 for the other sleeve.

19. Press fusible web tape along the front openings.

20. Remove the paper backing, turn under 1" and press.

21. Turn under ½" along the bottom hemline and press.

22. Pin beaded trim on top of the pressed hem and stitch along the top and bottom edges of the trim tape, turning under the ends.

23. Mark the placement, then sew four buttonholes to the right side of the sweatshirt.

24. Sew the four buttons to the opposite side, matching the buttonholes.

25. Create bead accents by re-threading a number of beads removed from the leftover trim tape and sewing them to the bottom of buttonholes.

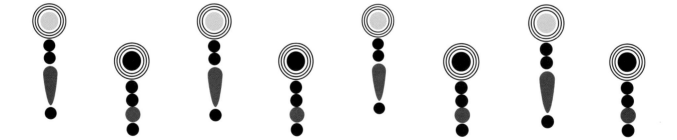

floral
chenille

Clothing items made from
or embellished with
chenille give the
illusion of warmth
and coziness.

Choose a more
sophisticated
look by using
chenille
in stylized
designs.

Materials

- Ivory sweatshirt
- 1 package of Chenille by the Inch
- Fusible web tape (½" wide)
- Fabric marker
- Hook and eye
- Light box
- Needle and thread
- Pins
- Scissors

Patterns

- Rose

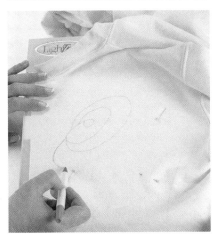

Trace the pattern onto the sweatshirt front.

Detail of the completed chenille trim.

Instructions

1. Remove the banding from the bottom of the sweatshirt.

2. Cut down the center of the sweatshirt front to create a cardigan (see page 11).

3. Press fusible web tape along the front opening and along the bottom hem.

4. Remove the paper backing from the fusible web tape and turn under 1" along the front opening and bottom hem. Press.

5. Stitch close to the raw edges of the hem and front opening. Repeat ¾" from the first row of stitching.

6. Using a light box and the rose pattern, trace the design onto the left front of sweatshirt.

7. Measure and mark parallel lines from the shoulder seam to the hem 2" and 3" from the left front edge. Do not trace the lines through the rose pattern.

8. Following the manufacturer's instructions, prepare and stitch Chenille by the Inch, beginning with the straight, parallel lines down the front of the sweatshirt.

9. Add a row of chenille along the neckline.

10. Stitch a hook and eye in place at the neckline edge.

Hints

If the color runs when laundered, use a laundry product designed to collect excess color.

Using different colors of chenille creates different looks. Be creative! Brighter colors may make the sweatshirt the perfect companion in the Spring, while darker colors will keep you warm on those chilly Autumn evenings.

crazy quilt botanical

I enhanced the look of the quilt-look printed fabric with crazy quilt embroidery stitches. The effect is visually pleasing, providing texture to look at, while making for a fun and simple project.

Materials

- Navy sweatshirt
- 1 yd. faux quilt print fabric
- ¼ yd. coordinating print for the prairie points
- ⅛ yd. coordinating print for the sleeve banding
- 4 decorative hooks and eyes
- Embroidery thread and needle
- Needle and thread
- Pins
- Scissors

Patterns

- Front Facing

Cutting Instructions

Faux quilt print fabric
- Cut two Front Facings.

Coordinating print for the prairie points
- Cut 2" squares for the prairie points. I used 28 total for my sweatshirt, but you may want to cut extra to account for the differences in sweatshirts.

Coordinating print for the sleeve banding
- Cut two 2" x 10" strips.

Hint

Adjust the width of the pattern to extend further onto the sweatshirt to accommodate the print, if needed.

Instructions

1. Cut the banding from the bottom of the sweatshirt.
2. Cut down the center of the sweatshirt front to create a cardigan (see page 11).
3. Create prairie points from the 2" squares cut from the coordinating print fabric for the prairie points (see page 22).
4. Turn under ½" along the outside edge of the facing and press.
5. Pin the right side of the fabric facing to the wrong side of the front of the sweatshirt, matching the front seam and the neckline.
6. Stitch the facing with ¼" seam down the front of the sweatshirt. Turn the facing to the right side and press.
7. Pin the facing in place on the front of the sweatshirt.
8. Baste along the neckline, outside edge and bottom of the facing.
9. Pin the prairie points in place along the neckline ¼" above the neckline seam line, where the banding is sewn to the sweatshirt. Adjust the points to fit the circumference of the neckline.
10. Pin the prairie points, then baste them in place.
11. Sew close to the edge of the prairie points.
12. Fold the neckline banding back over the raw edges of the prairie points and stitch in place by hand.

Pin the ribbed banding over the top of the prairie points along the neckline.

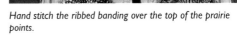

Hand stitch the ribbed banding over the top of the prairie points.

13. Use the two 2" x 10" strips from the coordinating fabric for the sleeve banding for an accent band on the sleeve. Turn under ½" along both sides the length of each sleeve banding strip. Press.

14. Place the prairie points just above the cuff seam. Adjust the points to fit the circumference of the sleeve. Pin, then baste in place.

15. Starting at the sleeve seam, place the sleeve banding fabric on top of the prairie point raw edges.

16. Trim the banding to fit, allowing for a 1" overlap.

17. Fold under 1" of fabric and finish the end. Pin, then baste the banding over the prairie points.

18. Topstitch two rows through all of the layers, staying parallel to the bottom edge.

19. Turn under 2" along bottom hem and press.

20. Open up the hem and press under ½". Pin in place.

21. Stitch close to the folded edge, starting at the fabric front facing.

22. Stitch a second row ⅛" away.

23. Select a section of fabric suitable for an appliqué on the back of the sweatshirt.

24. Cut out the appliqué and turn it under ½" on all sides. Press.

25. Pin the appliqué in place on the center of the back of the sweatshirt. Baste it in place.

26. Sew the decorative hook and eyes to the front of the sweatshirt.

27. Embellish the front, back and sleeves with embroidery stitches using the embroidery thread and needle. (see page 27). Be sure to secure the edges of facings and appliquès by stitching through the sweatshirt fabric.

asian poppy
redwork

The asymmetrical opening gives an Asian feel to this sweatshirt and the poppies add the right detail. Redwork, or backstitching, is a simple way to embroider a design. I added beads for that extra punch.

Materials

- White sweatshirt
- ¾ yd. fabric for the binding
- Black glass beads, size E
- Fabric marker
- Light box
- Red pearl cotton, size 8
- Embroidery needle
- Velcro
- Needle and thread
- Pins
- Scissors
- Tissue paper

Patterns

- Poppies

Cutting Instructions

Fabric for the binding

- Create a continuous bias binding (see page 21).
- Create a continuous bias ruffle (see page 22).

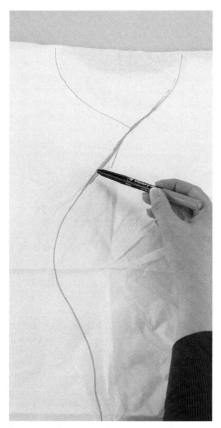

Draw a gentle curve on the tissue paper first.

Instructions

1. Remove the banding from the bottom and neckline of the sweatshirt.
2. Stay stitch along the cut edges. **Do not** cut the sweatshirt front open.
3. Fold the sweatshirt in half to mark the center front and press. At the same time, press a crease along the sides of the sweatshirt.
4. Cut a 4" slit up from the bottom edge at each side seam.
5. Open the sweatshirt and measure down 4" along the center fold line from the top and place a pin.
6. Using a piece of tissue paper, lay it on top of the sweatshirt.
7. Draw a gentle curve from the shoulder seam at the neckline to the pin mark then continue curving toward the bottom hem along the fold.
8. If you are satisfied with the curve, cut the sweatshirt.
9. Stay stitch along the cut edges of the front opening.
10. Press under ½" on one end of the gathered bias trim and lay the trim with right sides together on top of the sweatshirt, starting at the pin mark and matching the edges.
11. Gently pull the threads to gather the trim and pin in place along the curved edging around the neck and down the opposite side.
12. Press under ½" at the end of the strip to finish. Stitch with ½" seam.
13. Fold it to the inside of the sweatshirt. Topstitch two rows through all thicknesses running parallel to the curve.
14. Using the bias binding, enclose the bottom hem, stitching the binding up the side slits and pivoting back down the other side continuing around the sweatshirt. Fold the right sides of side slits together and stitch.
15. Using the light box, transfer the Poppies pattern onto the sweatshirt.
16. Complete the design using a redwork, or back stitch (see page 27).
17. Sew beads to the center of each flower.
18. Sew Velcro closures to each side of front of sweatshirt, overlapping one side over the other.

Detail of the finished neckline and front opening.

Detail of the redwork poppies.

navy zippered jacket

The basic design of a sweatshirt can be transformed into a wardrobe essential. The asymmetrical yoke and pocket placement give this sweatshirt an interesting look. The zippered opening and button tabs finish the design nicely.

Materials

- Navy sweatshirt
- ¾ yd. print fabric for the facing and pockets (A)
- ¾ yd. print fabric for the lining and bias binding (B)
- 3 buttons (½")
- 22" separating zipper
- Needle and thread
- Pins
- Scissors

Patterns

- Yoke
- Pocket

Cutting Instructions

Print fabric A
- Cut two yokes.
- Cut two pockets.

Print fabric B
- Cut two pockets.
- Create a continuous bias binding (see page 21).

Instructions

1. Remove the banding from the bottom of the sweatshirt.
2. Cut down the center of the sweatshirt front to create a cardigan (see page 11).
3. Pin the yokes, matching the shoulder seams right sides together. The facing should be positioned to extend over the back of the sweatshirt.
4. Stitch along shoulder seam with ½" seam. Fold the facing to the front and press.
5. Match the front seam and neckline edge. Trim the facing to fit along the neckline where the banding is attached to the shirt (see the photo).
6. Baste the facing along the neckline.
7. Topstitch a section of bias binding, covering the raw edge of the facing along neckline and bottom edge of facing, folding the ends to finish.
8. Lay the pocket sections together, right sides out. Using the bias binding, encase the raw edges to finish the top of both pockets.
9. Position the pockets in place starting at the front seams, continuing around the back. Pin in place.
10. Stitch along the lines marked on the pattern piece to create pockets.
11. Baste the zipper in place on the front edges of the sweatshirt.
12. Using a 9" section of the bias binding, fold it in half lengthwise and topstitch to create the fabric binding for the button loops.
13. Cut the binding into three sections, 3" long.
14. Fold a 3" section in half and stitch it in place on the inside top edge of each pocket.
15. Sew the buttons to the sweatshirt using the loops as a guide for placement.
16. Pin the binding in place along the the bottom edge of the sweatshirt, starting at the front and working around the sweatshirt encasing the pockets.
17. Baste, then stitch the binding in place.
18. Stitch a second row along the bottom of the binding.
19. Finish the front edges with a close zigzag stitch.
20. Following the manufacturer's instructions, sew the zipper in the front seam.
21. Stitch the final button loop at the top of the zipper along the neckline.
22. Sew a button to the opposite side of the button loop.

Pin the yoke along the shoulder seam.

The yoke is ready for the bias trim.

Sew the zipper in the front of the sweatshirt.

view
from a
window

Choose your
favorite landscape
for the window
scenes and
enjoy the view.

Materials

- Blue sweatshirt
- ½ yd. landscape print fabric
- Fusible web tape (¼")
- Tracing wheel
- Transfer paper
- Newsprint or tissue paper
- Needle and thread
- Pins
- Scissors
- Pencil
- Pinking shears

Patterns

- Large Window Inset
- Small Window Inset

Stitch through all layers along the stitching lines.

With the sweatshirt right-side out, trim close to the stitching lines.

Instructions

1. Turn the sweatshirt inside out and lay it on a flat surface.

2. Center the Large Window Inset pattern on the wrong side of the back of the sweatshirt.

3. Slide the transfer paper between the pattern and the sweatshirt fabric and transfer the pattern lines with the pencil.

4. Press fusible web tape along all of the transfer lines. Use small pieces along the curve in the pattern. Remove the paper backing.

5. Using the pattern pieces as a guide, center the landscape print fabric on top of the pattern and choose a pleasing section of the fabric that will be seen through the "window." Cut the fabric 1" larger than the pattern on all sides.

6. Center the fabric right side down onto the center of the back of the sweatshirt over the fusible web tape. Press.

7. Lay the pattern on top of the centered fabric and check for proper alignment. Pin through all layers (sweatshirt, fabric and pattern) to prevent shifting.

8. Stitch through all layers along the stitching lines, following the pattern.

9. Trim the threads and turn sweatshirt right-side out.

10. Trim close to the stitching lines inside the window panel, leaving ⅛" on each side of the stitching line. Start by slitting the fabric near the center, being careful to cut through only the top layer of the sweatshirt fabric. Using pinking shears, trim the excess fabric close to the stitching on the inside of the sweatshirt.

11. Repeat the process using the small window pattern on the left front of the sweatshirt.

quilted floral

Choose one of the many double-sided quilted fabric designs available today and dress up your sweatshirt with the addition of cuffs, a facing and pockets.

Materials

- Green sweatshirt
- 1 yd. double-sided quilted fabric
- 1 package of double folded bias tape
- 11 buttons (½")
- Needle and thread
- Pins
- Scissors

Patterns

- Front Facing
- Pocket
- Cuff

Cutting Instructions

Double-sided quilted fabric

- Cut two front facings.
- Cut two pockets.
- Cut two cuffs.

Stitch down the length of the facing.

Detail of the button placement.

Instructions

1. Remove the banding from the bottom of the sweatshirt.
2. Cut down the center of the sweatshirt front to create a cardigan (see page 11).
3. With wrong sides together, pin the facing along the front seam of the sweatshirt.
4. Stitch the facing with ¼" seam. Clip the seams close to the stitching. Turn and press the facing to the right side of the sweatshirt.
5. Trim the fabric close to the neckline.
6. Baste the facing along the front and neckline edge. Continue basting the facing in place, turning under ¼" along the shoulder and front edges.
7. Encase the top and side edges of the pocket with the bias tape and stitch.
8. Position the pockets in place by laying them under the front facing ½". Pin in place.
9. Stitch down the length of the facing, being sure to catch the pocket in the seam.
10. Stitch the end of the pocket closed.
11. Pin the binding in place along the bottom edge of the sweatshirt, catching the bottom of the pocket.
12. Baste the binding in place, then sew a double line of stitching.
13. Stitch the cuffs together with ½" seam (see page 14).
14. Encase the top edge of the cuff with the bias binding.
15. With the wrong side of sweatshirt sleeve and the right side of cuff, insert the cuff into the sleeve, matching the seams, stretching the knit cuff to fit the fabric cuff and pin.
16. Stitch the cuff with ½" seam.
17. Clip and trim the seams. Turn and press. Finish the seamed edge of the fabric cuff using a close zigzag stitch.
18. Turn the cuff right-side out and fold it back over the sleeve. Repeat Steps 13 through 18 for the other cuff.
19. Sew the buttons in place on the cuffs and around the neckline.

children's fashions

This chapter is packed with fun designs and techniques to make that special garment for a loved one. Have fun by choosing fabrics that make you smile while keeping your loved one in mind. Fleece embellishments are simple and provide a wonderful addition to many of these designs.

pastel roses

Being the mother of two girls provided me the opportunity to incorporate pink and other wonderful, soft pastel colors into their lives whenever I had the chance. Fleece is so forgiving and simple to work with, it was a pure joy designing this sweet jacket.

Materials

- Pink sweatshirt
- ⅛ yd. mint fleece
- ⅛ yd. lavender fleece
- ⅛ yd. pink fleece
- Hook and eye
- Needle and thread
- Pins
- Scissors
- Scissors with a wavy blade (optional)

Patterns

- Collar
- Roses
- Leaves

Cutting Instructions

Mint fleece

- Cut two strips 1½" x the length of the front opening (cut with the wavy-blade scissors, if desired).
- Cut one strip 1" x the circumference of the sweatshirt neckline (cut with the wavy-bladed scissors, if desired).
- Cut eight leaves.

Pink fleece

- Cut six collar pieces.
- Cut two roses.

Lavendar fleece

- Cut six collar pieces.
- Cut six roses.

Instructions

1. Remove the banding from the bottom of the sweatshirt.
2. Cut down the center of the sweatshirt front to create a cardigan (see page 11).
3. Fold the two 1½" mint fleece strips in half, encasing the front seam, and pin.
4. Stitch the strips in place.
5. Trim the removed bottom banding to remove the stitching and cut it in half lengthwise.
6. Stitch the two pieces of the banding together end to end to create one long piece.
7. Fold the long piece in half, pressing gently.
8. Stitch two rows of gathering stitches close to the raw edges of the banding.
9. Fold in ½" on each end to provide a finished end and pin it in place along the bottom hem, pulling up threads to gather.
10. Stitch it to the bottom of the sweatshirt.
11. Finish the inside seam with a zigzag stitch.
12. Sew two pink collar pieces right sides together with ¼" seam. Turn it right-side out and press. Repeat for the remaining pieces. You should have three completed pink collar pieces.
13. Sew two lavendar collar pieces right sides together with a ¼" seam. Turn it right-side out and press. Repeat for the remaining pieces. You should have three completed lavendar collar pieces.
14. Place the collar pieces in place along the neckline edge, starting at the front and alternating colors. Once they are evenly spaced, pin them in place.
15. Stitch the collar pieces close to the banding edge.

Detail of the collar.

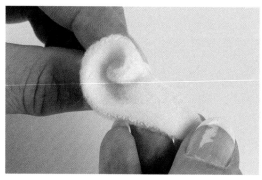

Roll the fabric between your fingers to make a rose.

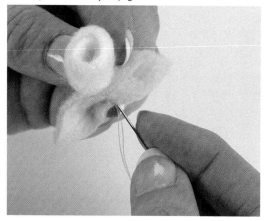

Sew a leaf to the bottom of the rose.

16. Stitch the 1" strip of mint fleece over the raw edge of the collar.

17. Fold the neckline banding over the top of the fleece and hand stitch it in place.

18. To make a rose, roll a lavendar piece between your fingers. Hand stitch it at the bottom (**do not** cut the thread).

19. Using the same uncut thread, weave through the middle of a mint fleece leaf and pull the thread taut. Repeat these steps for the remaining roses and leaves.

20. Stitch two roses to the front neckline and the remaining roses to the front of the sweatshirt.

21. Stitch a hook and eye in place at the neckline edge.

sweetheart
appliqué

Appliquéd hearts
and a scalloped
hemline
accented by a
crocheted trim
work wonderfully
together. Think of it as
a wearable Valentine.

Materials

- White sweatshirt
- ½ yd. print fabric
- ½ yd. fusible web
- 1 skein (50 gram) of curly eyelash yarn*
- Crochet hook, size G/6
- Variegated pink and red embroidery thread
- Embroidery needle
- Hook and eye closure
- Needle and thread
- 3" square of paper
- Pins
- Scissors
- Pencil

* Used in this project: Patons Cha Cha Yarn in BeBop

Patterns

- Heart
- Swirl

Cutting Instructions

Print fabric

- Cut as many hearts and swirls as you desire (I used six hearts and seven swirls), making sure to first apply fusible web to the wrong side of the print fabric.

Instructions

1. Remove the banding from the bottom of the sweatshirt.
2. Cut down the center of the sweatshirt front to create a cardigan (see page 11).
3. To make the scalloped hemline, start at the center back and mark a scalloped edge along the bottom hem (see page 19).
4. Trim the hem, turn under ¼" and press.
5. Press under ¼" along the front opening.
6. Using red embroidery thread, sew a blanket stitch at ¼" intervals along the front, bottom hem and seam line at the neckline and sleeve cuff (see page 27).
7. Single crochet along the neckline, front, hemline and cuffs (see page 26).
8. Remove the paper backing and fuse the appliqués in place on the front, setting one aside.
9. Fuse the remaining applique along the neckline on the back of the sweatshirt.
10. Sew a blanket stitch at ¼" intervals around all of the designs.

Detail of the crocheted trim.

strip-quilted vest

Why strip-quilting?
It's simple and the
characters on the
fabric are tumbling
at odd angles.
I felt the
feel of
the fabric
would be
lost if I cut
it into too
many pieces.

Materials

- Yellow sweatshirt
- 1 yd. print fabric
- ¼ yd. coordinating solid fabric (A)
- ¼ yd. coordinating solid fabric (B)
- 4 buttons (½")
- Needle and thread
- Rotary cutter, ruler and mat
- Fabric marking pen
- Pins
- Scissors

Cutting Instructions

Print fabric

- Cut three strips 1½" x the length of the fabric.
- Create a continuous bias binding (see page 21).

Coordinating solid fabric (A)

- Cut three strips 1½" x the length of the fabric.

Coordinating solid fabric (B)

- Cut three strips 1½" x the length of the fabric.

Instructions

1. Remove the banding from the bottom of the sweatshirt.
2. Cut off the sleeves plus an additional ½" around the inside edge of the armhole.
3. Cut down the center of the sweatshirt front to create a cardigan (see page 11).
4. Trim 2" off along the bottom of the sweatshirt.
5. To make the angular hemline, measure 4" from the bottom corner up the front of the sweatshirt and place a mark. Repeat along the bottom edge (see page 19).
6. Join the two dots with a ruler and draw a line.
7. Cut along this line. Repeat for opposite side.
8. On the right side of the sweatshirt, place a mark ½" down from the center point under the arm opening. Place a second mark at the center back along the hemline.
9. Draw a line from this point to the mark under the armhole, then to top of the neck seam line on the front of the sweatshirt. Pin the first strip of fabric along this line, right sides together.
10. Sew the strip with ¼" seam. Fold the fabric back over the seam and press well. Trim the excess fabric.
11. Matching the seam line, pin the second strip on top of the first strip right sides together.
12. Sew the second strip with ¼" seam. Press and continue working down the front of the vest until it is covered. Repeat on the opposite side.
13. Using the bias binding, finish all of the unfinished edges, mitering the corners for a neat finish. Use a zigzag stitch if desired. (To miter a corner, stitch toward the corner. When the needle is ¼" from the edge, stop stitching, leaving the needle in place. Raise the presser foot. Pivot the sweatshirt 45 degrees and tuck the excess binding under the stitching. Realign the binding and begin stitching.)

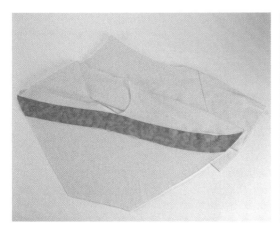

Sew the first fabric strip along the placement line.

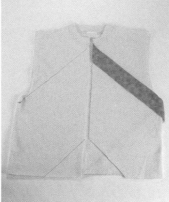

Fold the strip to the right side and press.

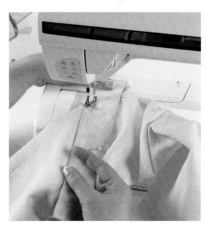

Sew the second strip on top of the first strip.

14. Roll the ribbed neckline banding to the inside leaving a scant ⅛" exposed and pin.

15. Topstitch through all layers parallel to the neckline edge.

16. To make the tie for the back of the vest, stitch a 16" piece of bias binding closed along the open edge.

17. Cut the strip in half.

18. On the back of the vest, measure 5½" up from the bottom edge and 3½" from the center on each side and place a mark.

19. Fold under ½" at the ends of the binding strip and stitch in place on top of the marks.

20. Trim the ends at an angle and tie in an overhand knot.

21. Cut a 16" section of bias binding.

22. Fold it in half lengthwise and topstitch.

23. Cut the binding into four 4" strips.

24. Fold each of the 4" sections in half and pin in place along the right side of the vest to create button loops.

25. Topstitch through all layers parallel to the vest front.

26. Stitch the four buttons on the opposite side of the vest using the loops as a guide for placement.

beach cover-up

The gentle ripples of the blue stripes on the fabric represented waves while bright umbrellas and fun beach buttons finished off the idea. Use this sweatshirt as a quick cover-up at the beach.

Materials

- White sweatshirt
- ¼ yd. tan fabric for the sand
- ¼ yd. blue fabric for the water
- ¼ yd. yellow fabric for the sun and drawstring tie
- Scraps of fabric for the umbrella
- 1 yd. fusible web
- Decorative buttons with a beach theme
- Needle and thread
- Measuring tape
- Pins
- Scissors

Patterns

- Umbrella
- Sun

Cutting Instructions

Tan fabric

- Cut one strip 4" x the length of the fabric for the sand, making sure to first apply fusible web to the wrong side of the fabric.
- Cut two strips 1" x the length of the front opening of the sweatshirt plus 1".

Blue fabric

- Cut one strip 5" x the length of the fabric for the water, making sure to first apply fusible web to the wrong side of the fabric.

Yellow fabric

- Cut one 1½" x 36" strip for the drawstring tie.
- Cut one Sun, making sure to first apply fusible web to the wrong side of the fabric.

Scrap

- Cut two Umbrellas, making sure to first apply fusible web to the wrong side of the fabric.

Instructions

1. Remove the banding from the bottom of the sweatshirt.
2. Cut down the center of the sweatshirt front to create a cardigan (see page 11).
3. Remove the paper backing from 4" strip of tan fabric and press it in place, running 8" parallel to the bottom edge of the sweatshirt.
4. Cut a curved line along the length of one side of the blue fabric.
5. Press the blue fabric over the bottom edge of the tan fabric.
6. Cut a wavy curve along the bottom hem of the sweatshirt.
7. Using a close zigzag or satin stitch setting on your machine, sew along the length of the tan, blue and bottom hemline.
8. Using a 1" strip of tan fabric, fold it over ½" at each end and ¼" along one side and press.
9. With right sides together, lay the fabric strip on the one side of the front opening of the sweatshirt and pin in place.
10. Stitch the strip with ¼" seam. Press it to the underside of the sweatshirt.
11. Once on the underside of the sweatshirt, stitch close to the folded edge. Repeat for the opposite side.
12. Fold over the neck banding to the right side of the sweatshirt and sew close to the edge, creating a casing.
13. Fold the 1½" x 36" strip of fabric in half lengthwise, right sides together.
14. Stitch the strip with ¼" seam. Turn it right-side out and press.

Detail of the drawstring neckline.

15. Thread the strip through the neckline casing and tie knots at each end.

16. Remove the paper backing and fuse the sun and umbrella appliqués to the front and back of the sweatshirt (see the photo for placement).

17. Using your sewing machine, satin stitch around all edges of the appliqués, continuing down from the umbrella to create a pole.

18. Sew the decorative buttons in place.

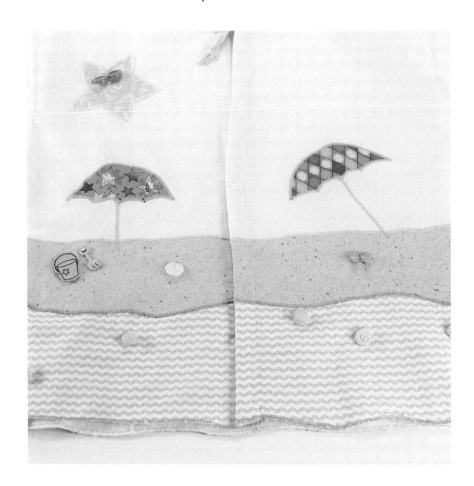

ribbons galore

The bright sunny colors and patterned ribbons are the base of this design. Simple vertical and diagonal stripes are stitched over the top of the ribbons, then fabric is cut away revealing the wonderful colors and patterns. Be sure to save the extra ribbon for matching hair accessories.

Materials

- Purple sweatshirt
- Assorted ribbons
- Fusible web tape (¼" wide)
- Fabric marking pen
- Ruler
- Needle and thread
- Scissors
- Pins

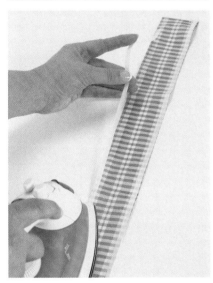

Press fusible web tape to the front of the ribbon trim.

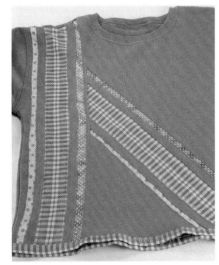

Encase the bottom edge of the sweatshirt with ribbon.

Instructions

1. Remove the banding from the bottom of the sweatshirt. This design is not a cardigan style. **Do not** cut down the center.

2. Turn the sweatshirt inside out and place it on a flat surface with the front of the sweatshirt face-up.

3. With the sweatshirt facing you, lay three ribbons vertically from the shoulder seam to the hem on the left side. Mark their placement with the fabric marking pen.

4. Starting at the bottom of the opposite corner, lay three more ribbons from that corner up to the lines for the vertical ribbons. Continue marking lines depending of the width of the ribbons.

5. Press fusible web tape to the right side of the ribbons, close to both edges.

6. Remove the paper backing and press the right side of the ribbons to the wrong side of the sweatshirt along the placement lines.

7. Stitch close to the ribbon edges.

8. Finish the ends of the ribbons by stitching them to the shoulder seam. Trim the excess ribbon and turn the sweatshirt right-side out.

9. Cut close to the stitching lines on the outside of the sweatshirt, revealing the ribbons. Be sure not to cut between the ribbons.

10. To make the hem binding, press a section of ribbon in half lengthwise.

11. Encase the bottom edge of the sweatshirt with ribbon, turning the ends under. Pin through all layers and stitch.

fleece kites

Simple fleece shapes are transformed into free-spirited kites swirling in the wind. The 3-D tails and strings drape gently to open hand buttons.

Materials

- Yellow sweatshirt
- ¼ yd. rainbow print fleece
- Fusible web tape (½" wide)
- Embroidery thread and needle
- Decorative buttons (hands)
- Needle and thread
- Scissors
- Pinking shears
- Pins

Patterns

- Large Kite
- Small Kite

Cutting Instructions

Rainbow print fleece

- Cut four Large Kites.
- Cut four Small Kites.
- Cut one 1" x 6" strip for the button loop.
- Cut eight ¾" x 1½" strips for the kite streamers.

Instructions

1. Remove the banding from the bottom of the sweatshirt.

2. Cut down the center of the sweatshirt front to create a cardigan (see page 11).

3. Press fusible web tape along the wrong side of front openings and bottom hem. Trim it with pinking shears.

4. Remove the paper backing from the fusible web tape and turn under ¾" along the front edges and 1" along the bottom hem. Press.

5. Pin the kites in place on the front of the sweatshirt, using the two large kites for elbow patches on the sleeves (see the photo for placement).

6. Using embroidery thread, blanket stitch at ¼" intervals around the kite appliqués (see page 27).

7. Using a chain stitch, embroider kite strings flowing freely down from the kite on the front of the sweatshirt (see page 27).

8. Stitch one ¾" x 1½" strip to each kite string, attaching it at the center to form a bow shape.

9. With right sides together, fold the 1" x 6" strip in half lengthwise and stitch it closed.

10. Turn the strip right-side out and stitch it to the outside of the neckline edge as a button loop.

11. Stitch the hand buttons along the string lines and one at the neckline edge, opposite the button loop.

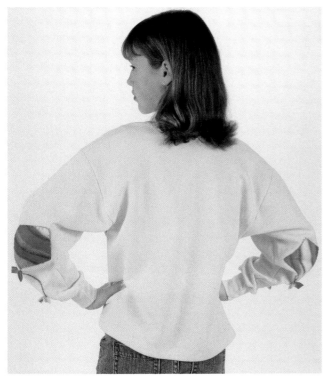

Detail of the kite elbow patches.

Detail of the kite appliqués and button details.

hooded chenille

Soft pinks and cozy chenille work perfectly together. The hood, pocket and embellishments are made from a remnant of chenille fabric.

Materials

- Pink sweatshirt
- ½ yd. chenille fabric
- ½ yd. fusible web
- Fusible web tape (½" wide)
- ½ yd. elastic (¼" wide)
- 1 skein (50 gram) chunky yarn*
- 1 package of white, single fold bias tape
- Crochet hook, size G
- Pink, yellow and pale blue embroidery thread
- Pearl and pale blue beads
- Needle and thread
- Scissors
- 3" piece of stiff cardboard
- Pins

* Used in this project: Sirdar Snowflake Chunky Magic

Patterns

- Hood
- Bear Face
- Muzzle
- Ears

Cutting Instructions

Chenille fabric

- Cut four hoods.
- Making sure to first apply fusible web to the wrong side of the fabric, cut the following pieces:
  one bear face
  two ears
  one 2" x 8" rectangle
  one 3½" square

Instructions

1. Remove the banding from the bottom of the sweatshirt.
2. Cut down the center of the sweatshirt front to create a cardigan (see page 11).
3. With right sides together, sew two hood sections together. Repeat with the second set.
4. Set one hood section inside the other, right sides together, matching the front edges.
5. Stitch the front edge with ¼" seam. Turn the hood right-side out and press.
6. Stitch the hood in place along the neckline where the ribbed binding meets the sweatshirt.
7. Fold the ribbed neckline banding over, covering the stitching line, and hand stitch in place.
8. Press fusible web tape along the bottom hem line and turn under 1" to the wrong side of the sweatshirt. Press well.
9. Topstitch the hem using the decorative wave stitch on your machine.
10. Measure 4" and 6" up from the cuff edge. Mark around the circumference of the sleeve at each measurement.
11. Cut along the 4" marking.
12. Press open the bias tape along the center fold.
13. Lay the white bias tape along the 6" mark, folding over the raw ends.
14. Stitch along both edges of the bias tape to create a casing.
15. Press under ¼" along the bottom of the sleeves and along the front openings.

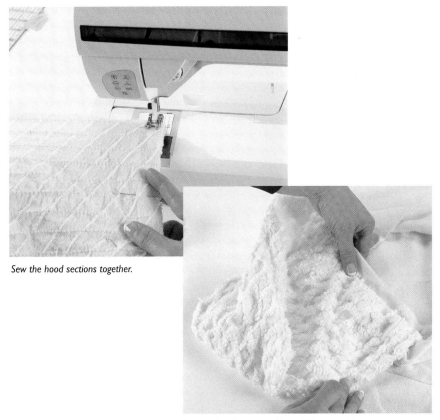

Sew the hood sections together.

Sew the hood to the neckline of the sweatshirt.

Detail of the front appliquéd trim.

16. Using matching embroidery thread, sew a blanket stitch at ¼" intervals along the front openings (see page 27).

17. Thread a 9" length of elastic through the casing on each sleeve. Stitch the ends together.

18. Cut open the leftover sections of the sleeves and press flat.

19. Cut a 5" x 5½" piece from the leftover sleeve to be used as the pocket.

20. Fold under ¼" along all sides of the pocket and sew a blanket stitch at ½" intervals using the matching embroidery thread (see page 27).

21. Single crochet one row along the front, bottoms of the sleeves and around the pocket (see page 26).

22. To make the tassel, use a 3" section of stiff cardboard and wrap the yarn around the cardboard 25 times.

23. Thread a 6" piece of yarn through the loops of yarn at the top and tie it tightly.

24. While holding onto the yarn tie, remove the loops from the cardboard and wrap another piece of yarn around the loops 1" down from the top. Tie a knot and trim the excess.

25. Cut the loops apart at the bottom of the tassel. Repeat for the second tassel.

26. Crochet two cord ties 6" in length using the chain stitch (see page 26).

27. Sew one end of the tie to the front of the sweatshirt at the neckline and attach the opposite end to the top of the tassels.

28. Cut the diamond shape and bear muzzle from the leftover sweatshirt fabric, making sure to apply fusible web to the fabric before cutting.

29. Remove the paper backing from the 3½" chenille square and iron it on the center of the pocket.

30. Satin stitch the edges of the chenille square and then pin the pocket in place on the lower left side of the sweatshirt.

31. Stitch close to the edges on three sides of the pocket.

32. Cut a point at the end of the 2" x 8" chenille rectangle and press it in place with the point inside the top edge of the pocket.

33. Center the diamond shape on top of the chenille rectangle. Press.

34. Use a close zigzag or satin stitch on your sewing maching to finish all the raw edges.

35. Press the ears, face and muzzle in place on top of the diamond.

36. Using embroidery thread, sew a blanket stitch around all the raw edges of the bear face (see page 27).

37. Use additional embroidery thread and beads as the eyes and nose accents.

animal bathrobe

This design provides a quick, inexpensive way to create a bathrobe. Find the perfect fabric, pick up a sweatshirt and you're almost there.

Materials

- Royal blue sweatshirt
- 1¼ yd. animal print fleece fabric
- Fabric marking pen
- Pins
- Needle and matching thread
- Measuring tape
- Pins
- Scissors

Patterns

- Hood

Cutting Instructions

Animal print fleece
- Trim the selvedge along one side of the fleece.
- Cut two strips 3½" x the length of the fleece.
- Cut one strip 3" x the length of the fleece.
- Cut one piece 1" x 8" for the belt loops.
- Cut one piece 23" x the width of the bottom hem of the sweatshirt.
- Cut four Hoods.

Instructions

1. Remove the banding from the bottom of the sweatshirt.
2. Cut down the center of the sweatshirt front to create a cardigan (see page 11).
3. Fold the large 23" length of fleece in half, right sides out.
4. Place a pin 3" from the top edge and 8½" out from the fold. Draw a line from the pin up to the top corner edge of the fleece on each side.
5. Lay the opened sweatshirt right-side up on a flat surface.
6. Center the fleece on top of the sweatshirt, overlapping the fleece over the bottom edge of the sweatshirt ½". Pin along the bottom of the sweatshirt and along the marked line.
7. Topstitch two rows through both layers following the marked lines and bottom edge of the sweatshirt.
8. Trim close to the stitching lines, removing excess fleece and sweatshirt fabric.
9. With right sides together, sew two hood sections together along the back seam line. Repeat with the second set.
10. Set one hood section inside the second with wrong sides together and baste along the front and neckline edge, starting at the left neckline edge where the binding meets the sweatshirt.
11. Pin, then stitch the hood in place along the binding edge using ¼" seam.
12. Fold over the banding to cover the stitching lines and hand stitch in place.
13. Sew the two 3½" strips of fleece together end to end to create one long piece.
14. Starting at the bottom front corner on the wrong side of the bathrobe, pin the fabric strips along the front edges around the hood and back down the opposite side.

Attach the fleece to the bottom of the sweatshirt.

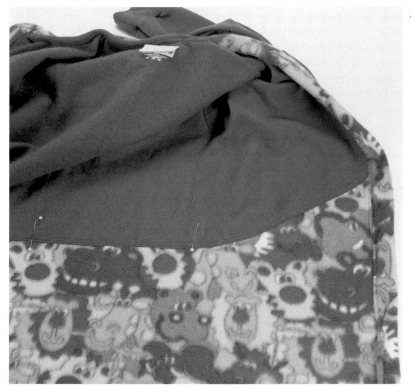

Thread the belt through the belt loops.

15. Stitch them in place.

16. Fold the banding to the front of the robe, covering the stitching line and sew in place close to the edge. Repeat ¼" away.

17. Fold the 3" strip of fleece in half lengthwise with wrong sides together and topstitch close to the edge. Repeat ¼" away from the first row of stitching. Trim the ends at an angle.

18. Fold the 1" x 8" strip of fleece in half lengthwise with wrong sides together and topstitch close to the edge.

19. Cut the strip in half to create two belt loops.

20. Sew the belt loops to the sides of robe, centering them over the 8½" pin placed at the side seams earlier.

about the author

Sewing has been a passion for most of Lorine's life, taking only short breaks when life took her down different paths. Her mother taught her the basics of sewing, but she is mostly self-taught, picking up knowledge through sewing books written by the experts. With her tendency to not follow instructions carefully combined with a sense of efficiency, she quickly developed shortcuts and a "what if" attitude. The thrill of hunting for the perfect fabric or embellishment is a favorite pastime.

During the past ten years, life once again took an interesting turn. Lorine designs using a variety of art mediums, and her work can be found in magazines, books and project sheets. She also enjoys teaching her crafts and projects. You might also find her designing and teaching children's art programs.

Lorine lives with the loves of her life: husband Bill, and two daughters, Jocelyn and Kimbrely, in Herndon, Va. Their journey to Virginia was a winding road that started in Winnipeg, Manitoba, where most of their families still reside. Each move can be traced by experiences that show up in her work from time to time.

resources

Beacon Adhesives
125 MacQuesten Parkway S.
Mount Vernon, NY 10550
(800) 865-7238
http://www.beaconcreates.com
Fabri-Tac™

Coats and Clark
P.O. Box 12229
Greenville, SC 29612-0229
(800) 648-1479
http://www.coatsandclark.com
Red Heart® Hokey Pokey™

Expo International, Inc.
5631 Braxton Drive
Houston, TX 77036
(800) 542-4367
http://www.expointl.com
Hairy gimp trim
Style #: IR2585 BG – Beige, BR – Brown

Fabric Café
12973-C Hwy. 155 So.
Tyler, TX 75703
(903) 509-5999
http://www.fabriccafe.com
Chenille by the Inch™

HTC Inc.
103 Eisenhower Parkway
Roseland, NJ 07668
2" Quilt Press™

HALCRAFT USA, Inc.
http://www.halcraft.com
Butterfly S Hook, Tea Pot and Spoon

Lion Brand® Yarn Company
(800) 258-9276
www.lionbrand.com
Chenille Thick & Quick® and Fun Fur

Patons®
P.O. Box 40
Listowel, ON Canada N4W 3H3
http://www.patonsyarns.com
Cha Cha and Twister yarns

SIRDAR Spinning Ltd.
http://www.sirdar.co.uk/
Snowflake Chunky Magic yarn

Sizzix®
25862 Commercentre Drive
Lake Forest, CA 92630-8804
(877) 355-4766
http://www.sizzix.com
Swirl diecut

The Warm™ Company
954 E. Union Street
Seattle, WA 98122
(800) 234-WARM
http://www.warmcompany.com
Steam A Seam 2®, Beads-2-Fuse™

Westwater Enterprises
Carlstadt, NJ 07072
(906) 654-9971
All natural handbag handles